D1288955

The Complete Illustrated
Children's Bible Dictionary

HARVEST
Kids

HARVEST HOUSE PUBLISHERS
EUGENE, OREGON

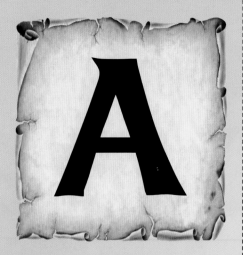

Aaron

The first priest of Israel. His story begins in Exodus, with Aaron as spokesperson for, and assistant to, his younger brother, Moses. Together they help to lead the Hebrews out of slavery and through years of desert wandering.

Abba

A Hebrew term of tender endearment by a beloved child who is in an affectionate, dependent relationship with his or her father. It is similar to "Papa" or "Daddy." "Because you are his sons, God sent the Spirit of his Son into our hearts, the Spirit who calls out, 'Abba, Father'" (Galatians 4:6).

Abednego

Abednego

Abednego is one of three Jewish men thrown into a blazing furnace by Nebuchadnezzar, king of Babylon, when they refused to bow down to his image. All three were preserved from harm (Daniel 3).

Abigail

Abel

Abel, a shepherd, is one of the sons of Adam and Eve. Cain, a farmer, kills his brother Abel in a jealous rage because God favored Abel's offering over Cain's (Genesis 4).

Abigail

Beautiful, wise Abigail was the wife of Nabal. She married David after Nabal's death, and together they had a son (1 Samuel 25).

Abner

The cousin of King Saul and commander of his army (1 Samuel 14:50).

Abram / Abraham

Abram means "exalted father." He was later known as Abraham, which means "father of many." Abraham, Isaac, and Jacob are the patriarchs of the nation of Israel.

A

Absalom
The third son of King David. He conspired to make himself king but was not successful.

Adam
In the story of creation, Adam was the first human, the father of humankind.

Aegean Sea
An arm of the Mediterranean Sea situated between the mainlands of Greece and Turkey.

Adonijah
The fourth son of King David, born at Hebron during the long conflict between David and King Saul.

Adoption
The legal process of becoming the parent of a child who is not one's own. God has adopted us as His children. "The Spirit you received does not make you slaves, so that you live in fear again; rather, the Spirit you received brought about your adoption to sonship. And by him we cry, 'Abba, Father'" (Romans 8:15).

Acts of the Apostles
After Luke wrote the Gospel of Luke, he wrote the book of Acts to show Jesus's ongoing ministry by the power of the Spirit through His church. In Acts we see the gospel spread from Jerusalem to much of the area around the Mediterranean Sea, and we see Christianity grow from a Jewish sect into an international faith. The book of Acts demonstrates that the gospel of salvation is for all because Jesus Christ is Lord of all.

A

Ahab
The seventh king of the northern kingdom of Israel. Jezebel was his wife. They were often at odds with Elijah the prophet.

Ahaziah
The seventh king of Judah and a relative of King Ahab of Israel.

Ahijah
An Israelite prophet of Shiloh from the tribe of Levi in the days of King Solomon. Ahijah encouraged a revolt against Solomon and prophesied that Jeroboam would become king of the northern kingdom of Israel (1 Kings 11:29-31).

Ai
The second city conquered by the Israelites in the Promised Land (Joshua 7). The ruins of the city are popularly thought to be in the modern-day archaeological site Et-Tell.

Almighty
All-powerful, omnipotent. "May God Almighty bless you and make you fruitful and increase your numbers until you become a community of peoples" (Genesis 28:3).

Altar
A table or flat-topped block used as the focus for a religious ritual, especially for making sacrifices or offerings. "The LORD appeared to Abram and said, 'To your offspring I will give this land.' So he built an altar there to the LORD, who had appeared to him" (Genesis 12:7).

Amalek
A grandson of Esau. Also, the nation that descended from him (also called Amalekites) and the territories they inhabited.

Amen
This word means "so be it" and is often said at the end of a prayer or sung at the end of a hymn.

Amnon
The oldest son of King David. He sinned against his sister Tamar and was killed by his brother Absalom.

Amorites
An ancient people from Syria who also occupied large parts of southern Mesopotamia from the twenty-first century BC to the end of the seventeenth century BC. They transformed several existing towns to prominent city-states, most notably Babylon.

Amorites

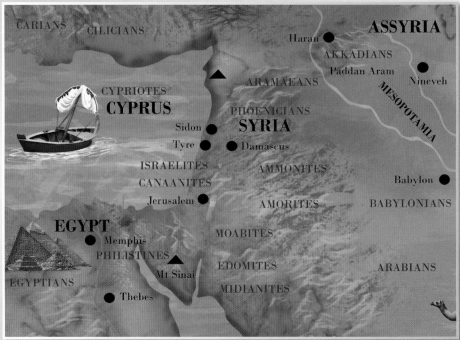

A

Amos

One of the 12 Old Testament minor prophets. An older contemporary of Hosea and Isaiah, he was active during the reign of Jeroboam II (786–746 BC). Amos was from the southern kingdom of Judah but preached in the northern kingdom of Israel on themes of social justice, God's omnipotence, and divine judgment. The book of Amos announces God's holy judgment on the northern kingdom of Israel, calling its people to repentance and encouraging them to turn from their self-righteousness and idolatry.

Ananias

Ananias and his wife, Sapphira, were members of the early Christian church in Jerusalem. They both died suddenly after lying to the Holy Spirit about money (Acts 5).

Another man named Ananias was sent by Jesus to restore the sight of Saul of Tarsus (later called the apostle Paul) and teach him about the way of the Lord (Acts 9).

Andrew

One of Jesus's apostles and the elder brother of Peter.

Angel

A spiritual being that acts as God's attendant, agent, or messenger. Angels are traditionally represented in human form.

Angel

Anger

A strong feeling of annoyance, displeasure, or hostility. "The LORD, the LORD, the compassionate and gracious God, slow to anger, abounding in love and faithfulness" (Exodus 34:6).

Anna

An elderly Jewish widow who prophesied about Jesus at the temple in Jerusalem (Luke 2:36-38).

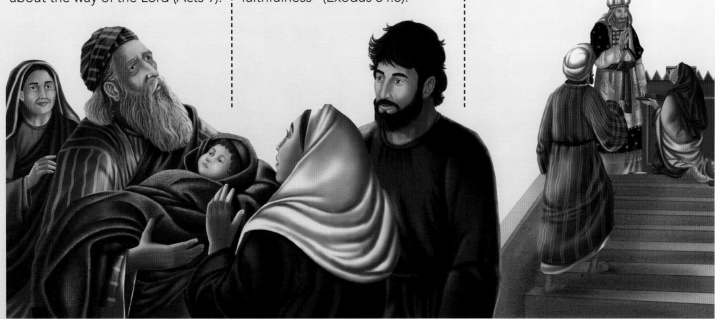

A

Anoint

To dab with oil or pour oil over, typically as part of a religious ceremony. "After you put these clothes on your brother Aaron and his sons, anoint and ordain them. Consecrate them so they may serve me as priests" (Exodus 28:41).

Antioch

An ancient Greco-Roman city on the eastern side of the Orontes River. Its ruins lie near the modern city of Antakya, Turkey.

Apostle

Someone sent with a special message or commission. Jesus is called "our apostle and high priest" in Hebrews 3:1. Jesus's first 12 apostles were Simon (Peter) and Andrew, James and John, Philip and Bartholomew, Thomas and Matthew, James the son of Alphaeus, Thaddaeus, Simon the Zealot, and Judas Iscariot (Matthew 10:2-4), who was replaced by Mathias (Acts 1:26). Paul became an apostle after Jesus's resurrection (2 Corinthians 1:1) along with Barnabas (Acts 14:14) and others.

Aquila and Priscilla

A first-century married couple who were Christian missionaries. They lived, worked, and traveled with the apostle Paul, who described them as his "co-workers in Christ Jesus" (Romans 16:3).

Aram

The name of three men in the Bible: a son of Shem (Genesis 10:22), a grandson of Nahor (Genesis 22:21), and an ancestor of Jesus (Ruth 4:19; 1 Chronicles 2:10; Matthew 1:3; Luke 3:33). In the Bible, Aram is also another name for Syria, the country lying to the northeast of Palestine.

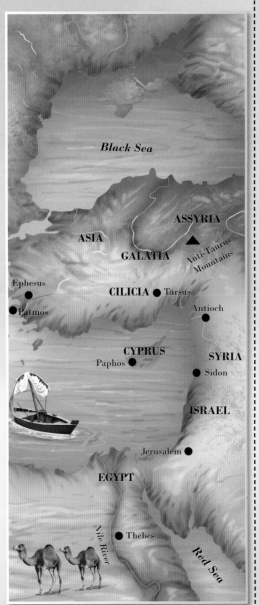

A

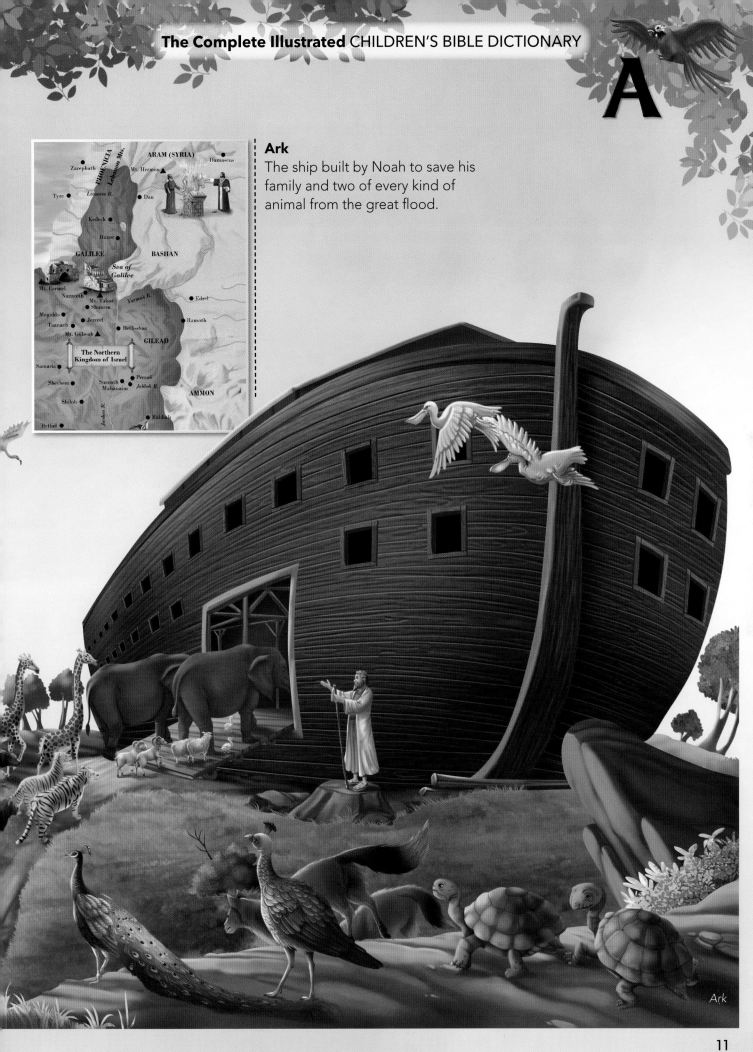

Ark
The ship built by Noah to save his family and two of every kind of animal from the great flood.

Ark

A

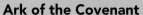

Ark of the Covenant

Also known as the Ark of the Testimony, this was a gold-covered wooden chest that was kept in the Old Testament tabernacle (and then the temple). It contained the stone tablets of the Ten Commandments, Aaron's staff that budded, and a gold jar of manna (Hebrews 9:4). On top was the mercy seat, where God's presence was manifested.

Armor of God

This phrase comes from Ephesians 6:13: "Therefore put on the full armor of God, so that when the day of evil comes, you may be able to stand your ground, and after you have done everything, to stand." The armor includes the belt of truth, the breastplate of righteousness, the gospel of peace, the shield of faith, the helmet of salvation, and the sword of the Spirit, which is the word of God.

Artaxerxes

Artaxerxes I was the king of Persia from 465 BC to 424 BC and the third son of Xerxes I. He commissioned Ezra the priest and Nehemiah the governor to rebuild the Jewish community in Jerusalem.

Ascension

Christ's ascent into heaven on the fortieth day after His resurrection.

A

Ascension

Asia Minor
Also called Anatolia, this peninsula comprises most of the Asian part of modern Turkey and the Armenian highland. It is surrounded by the Black, Aegean, and Mediterranean Seas.

Assyria
A kingdom in northern Mesopotamia and one of the great empires of the ancient Middle East. It was located in what is now northern Iraq and southeastern Turkey. Assyria conquered the northern kingdom of Israel and repopulated the land.

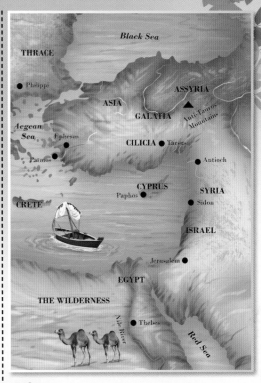

Athens
The capital of Greece and its largest city. It is one of the world's oldest cities.

Ark of the Covenant

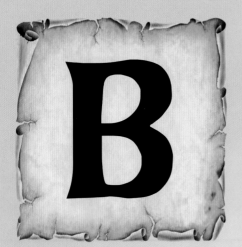

B

Baal

A Canaanite god. Israelites often sinned by worshipping Baal instead of the Lord.

Babel

The city of Babylon. The story of the tower of Babel is recorded in Genesis 11:1-9.

Babylon

The most powerful state in the ancient world after the fall of the Assyrian Empire in 612 BC. Its capital city, also called Babylon, was situated on the fertile plain between the Tigris and Euphrates rivers in ancient Mesopotamia. The city was beautifully adorned by King Nebuchadnezzar, who erected several famous buildings. The Babylonian army destroyed Jerusalem and Solomon's temple.

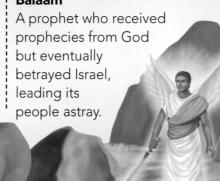

Balaam

A prophet who received prophecies from God but eventually betrayed Israel, leading its people astray.

Balaam

Balak

A king of Moab who summoned the prophet Balaam to prophecy against Israel (Numbers 22).

Baptism

A Christian rite of ceremonial cleansing with water, usually performed by sprinkling or immersion. It symbolizes a person's regeneration and admission to the Christian church.

Barabbas

A noted prisoner awaiting the death penalty when Jesus was arrested. It was a custom of the Roman government to release one Jewish prisoner at the yearly Passover festival. Pilate wanted to release Jesus, but the Jews demanded Barabbas (Matthew 27:16-26).

Barnabas

One of the prominent Jewish Christian disciples in Jerusalem. He befriended Paul when Paul was converted (Acts 9:27). When Barnabas was sent to Antioch, he took Paul with him (Acts 11:22-26). He undertook missionary journeys with Paul to spread the message of Christ and was called an apostle (Acts 14:14).

B

Bartholomew
One of Jesus's 12 apostles.

Bartimaeus
A man whom Jesus healed of blindness near Jericho (Mark 10:46-52).

Bathsheba
The wife of Uriah the Hittite. King David fell in love with her and had Uriah killed in battle. David married Bathsheba, and Solomon was one of their sons.

Beatitudes
The blessings listed by Jesus in the Sermon on the Mount (Matthew 5:3-11).

"Blessed are the poor in spirit, for theirs is the kingdom of heaven.
Blessed are those who mourn, for they will be comforted.
Blessed are the meek, for they will inherit the earth.
Blessed are those who hunger and thirst for righteousness,
    for they will be filled.
Blessed are the merciful, for they will be shown mercy.
Blessed are the pure in heart, for they will see God.
Blessed are the peacemakers, for they will be called children of God.
Blessed are those who are persecuted because of righteousness,
    for theirs is the kingdom of heaven."

B

Belshazzar

A co-regent of Babylon, governing the country after his father, King Nabonidus, went into exile in 550 BC. In 539 BC, Belshazzar held a great feast, during which he saw a hand writing on a wall. Daniel interpreted the writing as a judgment from God foretelling the fall of Babylon. Belshazzar died that very night, and Babylon fell to the Persians (Daniel 5).

Benjamin

The youngest of Jacob's thirteen children (twelve sons and one daughter) and the second and last son of Rachel. He is the father of the Israelite tribe of Benjamin.

Berea

A small Macedonian city now known as Veria. Paul, Silas, and Timothy preached the Christian gospel there, and the Bereans were commended for receiving the message and examining the Scriptures (Acts 17:10-12).

Bethany

A city near Jerusalem and the home of Mary, Martha, and their brother Lazarus.

Bethel

A border city located between Benjamin and Ephraim. Its name means "house of God." It was located where Jacob had a dream of angels ascending and descending on a ladder or stairway reaching to heaven (Genesis 28:10-12).

Bethesda

A pool "in Jerusalem near the Sheep Gate," where Jesus healed a man who had been an invalid for 38 years (John 5:2-9).

Bethlehem

The birthplace of King David and Jesus Christ, and the scene of a number of important events in biblical history.

Birds

God is sometimes pictured as a bird. "He will cover you with his feathers, and under his wings you will find refuge; his faithfulness will be your shield and rampart" (Psalm 91:4). Likewise, God's people are promised, "Those who hope in the LORD will renew their strength. They will soar on wings like eagles" (Isaiah 30:31).

B

Blood

In the Bible, blood is considered the essence of life and a requirement for atonement. "The life of a creature is in the blood, and I have given it to you to make atonement for yourselves on the altar; it is the blood that makes atonement for one's life" (Leviticus 17:11).

Boaz

A wealthy landowner of Bethlehem. He noticed Ruth, the widowed Moabite daughter-in-law of Naomi, gleaning grain in his fields. When he learned of her difficult circumstances and her loyalty to Naomi, Boaz invited her to eat with him and his workers, and he deliberately left grain for her to claim on his land. They eventually married, and King David was their great-grandson.

Born Again

This phrase from John 3 describes the experience of receiving new life through faith in Jesus Christ.

Bread

Jesus calls himself the bread of life. As bread helps sustains physical life, so Jesus provides eternal life. "I am the bread of life. Whoever comes to me will never go hungry, and whoever believes in me will never be thirsty" (John 6:35).

Bulrush

A tall, reedlike water plant with green leaves and a dark-brown, velvety, cylindrical head made up of lots of tiny flowers. "When [Moses's mother] could hide him no longer she took for him a basket made of bulrushes, and daubed it with bitumen and pitch; and she put the child in it and placed it among the reeds at the river's brink" (Exodus 2:3 RSV).

Burning Bush

On Mount Horeb, God spoke to Moses out of a bush that was on fire but was not consumed. He appointed Moses to lead the Israelites out of Egypt and into Canaan (Exodus 3).

Book of Life

The names of people who will inherit the gift of everlasting life (Revelation 3:5; 20:12).

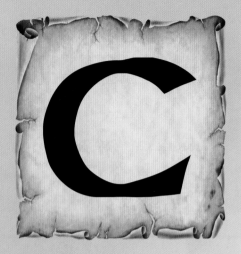

C

Caesar

Luke 2:1 tells us that Caesar Augustus, the first emperor of the ancient Roman Empire, ordered that a census be taken of the entire Roman world, possibly for tax purposes. In doing so, he paved the way for Jesus to be born in Bethlehem, fulfilling a biblical prophecy made 600 years before he was born.

Caesarea

In the first century, Caesarea was a major Roman political center in Israel. It was built between 25 and 13 BC by Herod the Great, who named it after Caesar Augustus. Caesarea was located on the shore of the Mediterranean Sea, on the road from Egypt to Tyre, about 75 miles northwest of Jerusalem.

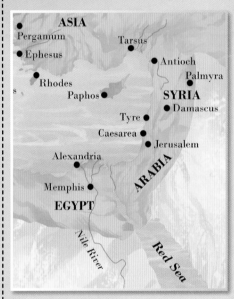

Caesarea Philippi

Situated at the base of Mt. Hermon, 25 miles north of the Sea of Galilee, Caesarea Philippi was an ancient Roman city and home to one of the largest springs feeding the Jordan River. This is where Peter said to Jesus, "You are the Messiah, the Son of the living God" (Matthew 16:16).

Caiaphas

A Jewish high priest who helped organize the plot to kill Jesus.

Cain

One of the sons of Adam and Eve. He killed his brother Abel because God favored Abel's sacrifice (from his flock) over Cain's sacrifice (from his crops). God condemned Cain to be "a restless wanderer on the earth," but He lightened Cain's punishment after Cain complained that it was too difficult to bear (Genesis 4).

Caleb

A representative of the tribe of Judah during the Israelites' journey to the Promised Land. He and Joshua were two of the 12 spies sent into Canaan to explore the land.

Calf

A young cow or bull in its first year. Israel included calves in their burnt offerings to God (Leviticus 9:3,8). A calf was also a symbol of peace and prosperity. "The wolf shall dwell with the lamb, and the leopard shall lie down with the young goat, and the calf and the lion and the fattened calf together; and a little child shall lead them. The cow and the bear shall graze; their young shall lie down together; and the lion shall eat straw like the ox" (Isaiah 11:6-7).

Camel

A large, long-necked mammal with long, slender legs; broad, cushioned feet; and either one or two humps on its back. Camels are well adapted to live in hot, dry climates because they can survive for long periods without food or drink, chiefly by using up the fat reserves in their humps. "It is easier for a camel to go through the eye of a needle than for a rich person to enter the kingdom of God" (Matthew 19:24).

Cana

A town in Galilee where Jesus performed His first miracle, turning water into wine at a wedding feast (John 2).

Canaan

A large area on the east side of the Mediterranean Sea that provides the main setting for the stories in the Old Testament. It was originally home to the Philistines and other indigenous groups, but God promised it to Abraham and his descendants (Genesis 15:7). It was named after a grandson of Noah (Genesis 10:15-19) and corresponds roughly to present-day Lebanon, Syria, Jordan, and Israel.

Capernaum

A fishing village on the northern shore of the Sea of Galilee and the hometown of the apostles Peter, James, Andrew, John, and Matthew. When Jesus was rejected at His hometown of Nazareth, He made Capernaum a base of operations.

Cattle

This term can refer to animals related to domestic cattle, including yak, bison, and buffaloes. "For every beast of the forest is mine, the cattle on a thousand hills" (Psalm 50:10).

Camel

C

Census

A count of the entire population of an area. "In those days Caesar Augustus issued a decree that a census should be taken of the entire Roman world" (Luke 2:1).

Centurion

The commander of a century (30 or 60 soldiers) in the ancient Roman army. "Jesus said to the centurion, 'Go! Let it be done just as you believed it would.' And his servant was healed at that moment" (Matthew 8:13).

Chariot

A type of carriage pulled by horses. "[The king of Egypt] had his chariot made ready and took his army with him. He took six hundred of the best chariots, along with all the other chariots of Egypt…so that he pursued the Israelites, who were marching out boldly" (Exodus 14:6-8).

Christ

The Messiah, the Deliverer and King that the Jews expected. Christians believe that Jesus is the Christ. "To you is born this day in the city of David a Savior, who is Christ the Lord" (Luke 2:11 RSV).

Christian

A follower of Jesus Christ. "The disciples were called Christians first at Antioch" (Acts 11:26).

Church

In the Bible, the church is not a building. Sometimes the word refers to all of Christ's followers (Matthew 16:18), and sometimes it refers to a smaller, local group of believers (Acts 14:23).

Colossae

A city in ancient Phrygia, which was part of the Roman territory of Asia Minor. The apostle Paul's New Testament letter to the Colossians lifts up Christ as the image of God, warns against legalism and asceticism, and promises union with Christ.

"God has chosen to make known among the Gentiles the glorious riches of this mystery, which is Christ in you, the hope of glory" (Colossians 1:27).

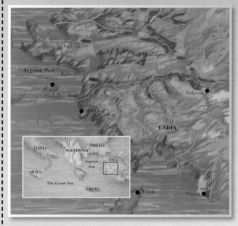

Commandment

In the Bible, this word refers to a divine rule, such as one of the Ten Commandments (Exodus 20) or one of Jesus's directives. "A new command I give you: Love one another. As I have loved you, so you must love one another" (John 13:34).

Communion

This word does not appear in most Bible versions, but it commonly refers to the Christian sacrament that Jesus instituted at the last supper (1 Corinthians 11:23-26).

Compassion

Sympathy, pity, and concern for the sufferings or misfortunes

C

of others. "As a father has compassion on his children, so the LORD has compassion on those who fear him" (Psalm 103:13).

Confess
To admit that one has done something wrong. "Confess your sins to each other and pray for each other so that you may be healed. The prayer of a righteous person is powerful and effective" (James 5:16).

Corinth
An ancient and celebrated city of Greece, about 40 miles west of Athens. The apostle Paul visited Corinth at least three times, with one visit lasting a year and a half (Acts 18:11). He wrote several letters to the church there, and two of those letters are in the New Testament.

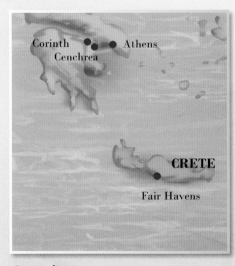

Cornelius
A Roman centurion and the first Gentile to become a Christian (Acts 10).

Covenant
An agreement or contract. God made covenants with Noah, Abraham, Moses, and David. God promised to make a new covenant with His people (Jeremiah 31:31), which He did through Jesus (1 Corinthians 11:25).

Crete
The largest and most populous of the Greek islands, and the fifth-largest island in the Mediterranean Sea.

The Mediterranean Sea

Cross
The wooden structure on which Jesus was crucified. "'He himself bore our sins' in his body on the cross, so that we might die to sins and live for righteousness" (1 Peter 2:24). Figuratively, the word also refers to the struggles Jesus's followers face. "Then Jesus said to his disciples, 'Whoever wants to be my disciple must deny themselves and take up their cross and follow me'" (Matthew 16:24).

Crown
In the New Testament, crowns are symbols of rewards that God has promised to those who love and serve Him. "Blessed is the one who perseveres under trial because, having stood the test, that person will receive the crown of life that the Lord has promised to those who love him" (James 1:21).

Crucifixion
An ancient form of execution in which a person was nailed or bound to a cross.

Cyprus
One of the largest islands of the Mediterranean. It was the home of Barnabas (Acts 4:36) and the scene of Paul's first missionary labors (Acts 13:4-12).

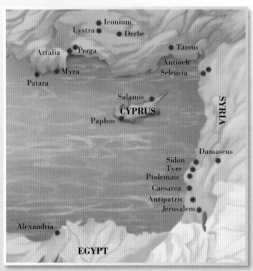

Cyrus
Cyrus the Great (559–530 BC) was king of Persia. Under his reign, the Babylonians were defeated and the captive Jews were allowed to return to Jerusalem and rebuild the temple.

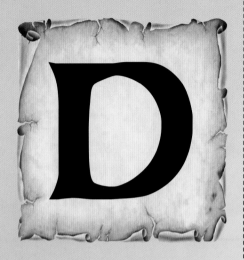

Damascus

The capital of Syria (also called Aram in the Bible) and one of the oldest cities in the Middle East.

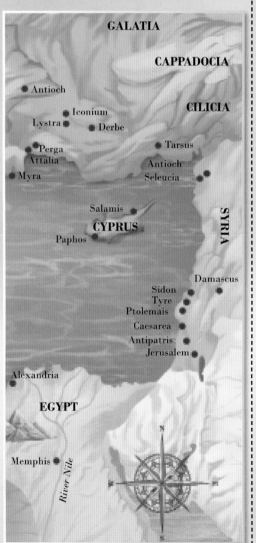

Dan

The fifth son of Jacob and the father of the Israelite tribe of Dan.

Daniel

A young Jew who was taken into captivity by Nebuchadnezzar of Babylon and served the king and his successors until the time of the Persian conqueror Cyrus. All the while, Daniel remained true to the God of Israel.

The Old Testament book that bears his name is most famous for the stories of Daniel in the lions' den and the account of Shadrach, Meshach, and Abednego in the blazing furnace. It also includes prophecies that many Christians believe apply to the end times.

Darius

The name of several Persian kings:

- Darius the Mede (Daniel 11:1), who was king when Babylon was conquered and when Daniel was thrown in the lions' den
- Darius, king of Persia (Ezra 4), who tried to stop the Jews from rebuilding the temple
- Darius the Persian (Nehemiah 12:22)

David

The second and greatest king of Israel, reigning from about 1010 to about 970 BC. David was a brave warrior and the composer of many psalms. He is described as a man after God's own heart in 1 Samuel 13:14 and Acts 13:22.

D

Day of Atonement

Known today as Yom Kippur, this is the holiest day of the Jewish year. In the Old Testament, it was the one day the high priest was to enter the Most Holy Place and make atonement for the sins of the people (Leviticus 16).

Dead Sea

A salt lake bordered by Jordan to the east and Israel and Palestine to the west. Also known as the Salt Sea or the Sea of the Arabah, this inland body of water has such a high mineral content that nothing can live in its waters.

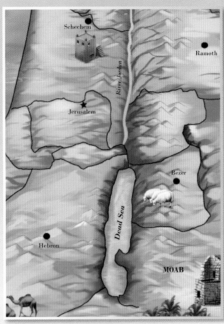

Death

The apostle Paul described death as "the last enemy to be destroyed" by Christ (1 Corinthians 15:24-26). Jesus shared in our humanity "so that he might break the power of him who holds the power of death—that is, the devil—and free those who all their lives were held in slavery by their fear of death" (Hebrews 2:14-15).

Deborah

The only female judge and the only judge to be called a prophet. She is a decisive figure in the defeat of the Canaanites (Judges 4–5).

Delilah

Samson's lover and the master of his downfall (Judges 16).

Demon

An evil, supernatural being, often considered to be a fallen angel. "These signs will accompany those who believe: In my name they will drive out demons" (Mark 16:17).

Derbe

A city in the district of Lycaonia, in the Roman province of Galatia, in south central Asia Minor. Paul and Barnabas fled to Derbe and Lystra during Paul's first missionary journey when the city officials of Iconium plotted to stone them (Acts 14:6-21).

Delilah

D

Deuteronomy

The fifth book of the Old Testament, consisting of three sermons or speeches Moses delivered to the Israelites on the plains of Moab shortly before they entered the Promised Land. Moses recounts the 40 years of wilderness wandering and encourages the Israelites to worship just one God and observe the laws and teachings He has given them so they can possess the land.

Devil

A supernatural being, likely a fallen angel, who is the primary opponent of God. The word means "slanderer" or "accuser." He is often identified as the serpent who tempted Eve in Eden (Revelation 12:9; 20:2). He will be condemned to the lake of fire (Revelation 20:10).

Discipline

The ability to control yourself, even in difficult situations (2 Timothy 1:7). Also, training that corrects and shapes the character. "No discipline seems pleasant at the time, but painful. Later on, however, it produces a harvest of righteousness and peace for those who have been trained by it" (Hebrews 12:11).

Donkey

The Bible includes two well-known stories about donkeys. One donkey spoke to the prophet Balaam (Numbers 22:21-31), and the other carried Jesus into Jerusalem the week of His crucifixion (Matthew 21:1-11).

Doorpost

God directed the Israelites to put a lamb's blood on the doorposts of their houses. He said that when He judged Egypt, He would see the blood and pass over their houses (Exodus 12).

Dove

Noah sent a dove from the ark to search for dry ground (Genesis 8:8-12). Doves were used as sacrifices when people could not afford lambs (Leviticus 5:7). And the Holy Spirit descended on Jesus like a dove (Matthew 3:16).

Dreams

In the Bible, God sometimes spoke to people in dreams. He also empowered Joseph and Daniel to interpret other people's dreams. And He promised, "I will pour out my Spirit on all people. Your sons and daughters will prophesy, your old men will dream dreams, your young men will see visions" (Joel 2:28). Peter preached that this prophecy was fulfilled on the Day of Pentecost (Acts 2:14-17).

Earth

The Bible teaches that the earth is good (Genesis 1:9-10). It is currently subject to decay, but it will be liberated someday (Romans 8:18-21).

Easter

This word does not appear in most Bible versions, but Easter is the most important and oldest festival of the Christian church, celebrating the resurrection of Christ. In the Western church, Easter falls on the first Sunday after the first full moon following the northern spring equinox.

Ecclesiastes

This word means "teacher" or "preacher," which is what the author of the book of Ecclesiastes calls himself. He also introduces himself as "son of David, king in Jerusalem" (that is, Solomon), and he goes on to discuss the meaning of life and the best way to live. The book concludes with this injunction: "Fear God and keep his commandments, for this is the duty of all mankind" (12:13).

Eglon

One of the rulers of Moab who oppressed the Israelites. He is known for being "a very fat man" (Judges 3:17).

Egypt

A country that links northeast Africa with the Middle East. It was where Israel grew from a single family into a nation of slaves. God struck Egypt with ten plagues because Pharaoh refused to set the Israelites free (Exodus 7–11).

Ehud

A left-handed judge who was sent by God to deliver the Israelites from Moabite domination (Judges 3:12-30).

E

Elder

In the Old Testament, elders are respected leaders of Israel. In the New Testament, elders are responsible for the leadership and oversight of churches. "Paul and Barnabas appointed elders for them in each church and, with prayer and fasting, committed them to the Lord, in whom they had put their trust" (Acts 14:23).

Eli

Eli was a high priest of Israel at Shiloh when Samuel was born and began to minister (1 Samuel 1–3).

Elijah

One of Israel's greatest prophets, Elijah operated in the northern kingdom of Israel during the reign of wicked King Ahab. Elijah performed many miracles. He never died, but was taken up to heaven in a whirlwind (2 Kings 2:11-12). Centuries later, Elijah appeared with Moses and Jesus on the Mount of Transfiguration (Matthew 17:1-3).

Elisha

Elijah's disciple and successor. Like Elijah, Elisha performed many miracles, including raising a dead boy back to life (2 Kings 4:8-37).

Elizabeth

A descendant of Aaron, the wife of Zechariah, and the mother of John the Baptist. Luke describes the couple as "righteous in the sight of God, observing all the Lord's commands and decrees blamelessly" (Luke 1:6).

Elijah

26

E

Emmaus

After His death and resurrection, Jesus appeared to two of His disciples while they were walking on the road to Emmaus (Luke 24:13-35).

Encouragement

Encouragement is one of the services Christians are to provide for one another. "Therefore encourage one another and build each other up, just as in fact you are doing" (1 Thessalonians 5:11). It is also a characteristic of prophecy. "The one who prophesies speaks to people for their strengthening, encouragement and comfort" (1 Corinthians 14:3).

Ephesians

Paul wrote this New Testament letter to the believers in Ephesus while he was imprisoned in Rome. It includes Paul's famous description of the armor of God (Ephesians 6:10-17).

Ephesus

A center of travel and commerce and one of the greatest seaports in the ancient world. Timothy and John were both leaders in the church there, but by the end of the first century, many in the church had lost their first love (Revelation 2:4).

Ephraim

A son of Joseph and the father of the Israelite tribe of Ephraim.

Epistles

New Testament letters. Of the 27 books in the New Testament, 21 are epistles. The word "epistle" comes from the Greek word *epistole*, meaning "letter" or "message."

Esau

One of Isaac and Rebekah's twin sons, born just before Jacob, who was holding Esau's heel. His name means "hairy" or "rough." He was also called Edom ("red") because of his red hair. He was the patriarch of the nation of Edom.

Esther

Esther, born Hadassah, is the heroine of the book of Esther. A Jewish orphan, she was raised by her cousin Mordecai and eventually became queen of King Xerxes of Persia. She saved Israel from annihilation, an event celebrated in the Jewish festival of Purim.

Ethiopian Eunuch

The treasurer of Candace, the queen of the Ethiopians. One day, as he was reading from the prophet Isaiah in his chariot, he was met by Philip, who had been sent by the Holy Spirit from Samaria to help him. Philip told him the good news about Jesus, and the eunuch was baptized (Acts 8:26-40).

E

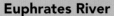

Euphrates River

The longest and one of the most historically important rivers of western Asia, first mentioned in Genesis 2:14 as one of the rivers of paradise.

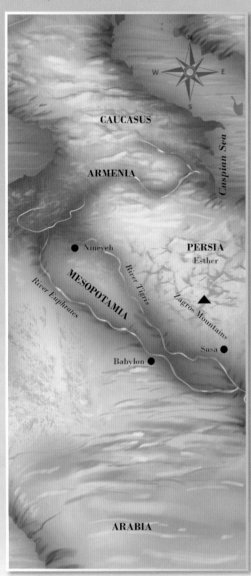

Eutychus

In Acts 20:7-12, Eutychus, a young man of Troas, falls asleep during one of the apostle Paul's long discourses. He topples from a windowsill, falling three stories into the street below. Paul embraces him, insisting that he is not dead, and carries him back upstairs alive.

Eve

The companion God makes for Adam. Adam named her Eve because "she would become the mother of all the living" (Genesis 3:20). "Eve" means "life."

Exodus

The second Old Testament book, written sometime between 1450 and 1410 BC. It records the events of Israel's deliverance from slavery in Egypt. It also contains the account of God giving Israel the Ten Commandments and other laws to guide them in their relationship with Him.

Ezekiel

A prophet and the central figure of the book of Ezekiel. Exiled in Babylon from 593 to 571 BC, he was the prophet who saw the vision of the dry bones.

Ezra

A scribe and priest who led a group of Judean exiles living in Babylon to their home city of Jerusalem in 538 BC. The Old Testament book of Ezra describes that journey and the completion and dedication of the second temple in Jerusalem in 513 BC.

Ezra

Faith

In the Bible, faith refers to the way we relate to God—by believing in Him, trusting Him, being committed to Him, and seeing the world the way He would have us see it. "By grace you have been saved, through faith—and this is not from yourselves, it is the gift of God" (Ephesians 2:8).

Fall

The disobedience of Adam and Eve, which led to their banishment from the Garden of Eden and the fall of humankind into a state of sin (Genesis 3).

Famine

A lack of food. The Bible mentions many famines. One of the most famous is the seven-year famine Joseph predicted while in Egypt. He saved the people by having them store up grain for seven years before the famine arrived (Genesis 41).

Father

In addition to a biological father, this word can refer to many people in the Bible, including…

- An ancestor (Matthew 3:9)
- A chief, ruler, or elder (2 Kings 2:12)
- The author or beginner of anything (Genesis 4:20-21)
- God (Matthew 6:9)

Feast

A large meal, typically eaten as part of a celebration. Israel had seven important feasts:

- Passover
- Unleavened Bread
- First Fruits
- Weeks (Pentecost)
- Trumpets
- Atonement
- Tabernacles (Booths)

Feeding the Five Thousand

Jesus used five barley loaves and two small fish to feed 5,000 men plus women and children (John 6:1-15).

Fiery Furnace

Jewish exiles Shadrach, Meshach, and Abednego were thrown into a fiery furnace by Nebuchadnezzar, king of Babylon, when they refused to bow down to his image. They were all saved from harm (Daniel 3).

Fish

Jesus performed at least five miracles with fish. Two of the miracles included huge harvests of fish after hours of catching nothing (Luke 5:4-6; John 21:6). Jesus instructed Peter to catch a fish and use the coin in its mouth to pay their taxes (Matthew 17:24-27). And Jesus fed two huge crowds with just a few loaves of bread and a few small fish (Matthew 14:13-21; 15:29-38).

Feeding the Five Thousand

F

Fleece
The warm, woolly covering of a sheep or goat. Gideon used a fleece to determine God's will (Judges 6:36-40).

Food
In the Old Testament, God miraculously fed the Israelites throughout their 40-year wilderness wanderings (Exodus 16). In the New Testament, Jesus said, "I am the living bread that came down from heaven. Whoever eats this bread will live forever" (John 6:51).

Foolishness
The lack of good sense or judgment. "The foolishness of God is wiser than human wisdom, and the weakness of God is stronger than human strength" (1 Corinthians 1:25).

Foot Washing
Jesus washed His disciples' feet at the Last Supper. He encouraged the disciples to follow His example of humble service (John 13:1-17).

Forgiveness
Choosing not to judge someone who has done something wrong. "Be kind and compassionate to one another, forgiving each other, just as in Christ God forgave you" (Ephesians 4:32). "Forgive as the Lord forgave you" (Colossians 3:13).

Frankincense
An aromatic gum resin obtained from an African tree and burned as incense. It was burned in the temple (Exodus 30:34-38) and given to the baby Jesus by the wise men (Matthew 2:11).

Friends
• "Abraham…was called God's friend" (James 2:23).

• "The Lord would speak to Moses face to face, as one speaks to a friend" (Exodus 33:11).
• "Anyone who chooses to be a friend of the world becomes an enemy of God" (James 4:4).

Fruit of the Spirit
The apostle Paul lists nine of the attributes of the Christian life: "The fruit of the Spirit is love, joy, peace, forbearance, kindness, goodness, faithfulness, gentleness and self-control" (Galatians 5:22).

Furnace
Shadrach, Meshach, and Abednego were threatened with being thrown into a furnace unless they worshipped the king of Babylon. But they replied, "If we are thrown into the blazing furnace, the God we serve is able to deliver us from it, and he will deliver us from Your Majesty's hand" (Daniel 3:17). Figuratively, the Bible refers to a difficult situation as a refiner's furnace. "See, I have refined you, though not as silver; I have tested you in the furnace of affliction" (Isaiah 48:10).

Gabriel

A messenger who was entrusted to deliver important messages from God to the prophet Daniel (Daniel 8:16), to the priest Zechariah (Luke 1:19), and finally to the Virgin Mary (Luke 1:26-38). Gabriel is the one who revealed that the Savior was to be named Jesus (Luke 1:31).

Gad

One of the sons of Jacob and the father of the Israelite tribe of Gad. Another man named Gad was a prophet to King David (1 Samuel 22:5).

Galatia

An area in modern Turkey. It was named for the immigrant Gauls from Thrace who settled there in the third century BC.

Galatians

One of the apostle Paul's New Testament letters. Paul warns the Galatians not to trust in the Law but to receive God's grace through faith.

Galilee

A region in northern Israel. Most of the events recorded in the first three Gospels occur in this province.

Gamaliel

A Pharisee who was held in great esteem by all Jews. He was the apostle Paul's teacher before Paul began following Christ (Acts 22:3), and he urged the Sanhedrin not to put the apostles to death (Acts 5:33-40).

Garden of Eden

The home of Adam and Eve before they sinned.

Garden of Gethsemane

An olive grove at the foot of the Mount of Olives in Jerusalem. Jesus prayed there while His disciples slept on the night before His crucifixion.

Gabriel

G

Gaza
Situated on the Mediterranean coast, Gaza is one of the oldest cities in the world. Samson carried away its gates (Judges 16:1-3), and he was held prisoner there until he died pulling down the temple of Dagon, killing "all the rulers of the Philistines" (Judges 16:23-30).

Genesis
Genesis (meaning "origin" or "in the beginning") is the first book of the Old Testament. It includes the stories of creation, the fall of mankind, Noah and the flood, the patriarchs (Abraham, Isaac, and Jacob), and Joseph's adventures in Egypt.

Gentile
A person of a non-Jewish nation or of non-Jewish faith. "I am not ashamed of the gospel, because it is the power of God that brings salvation to everyone who believes: first to the Jew, then to the Gentile" (Romans 1:16).

Giants
Giants are mentioned in the Bible in several places, including Genesis 6:4 (Nephilim) and Joshua 12:4 (Rephaites). Moses's 12 spies reported seeing giant people in Canaan (Numbers 13:30-33). Perhaps the most famous biblical giant is Goliath (1 Samuel 17:4), who was thought to be between seven and ten feet tall!

Gibeon
A Canaanite city north of Jerusalem that was conquered by Joshua and the Israelites.

Gideon
One of Israel's judges. With only 300 men, he defeated an entire Midianite army (Judges 7).

Gilgal
A settlement on the west of the Jordan where Israel spent their first night in the Promised Land after crossing the Jordan River.

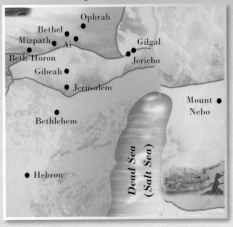

Gleaning
Collecting leftover crops from farmers' fields after they have been harvested. Some ancient cultures promoted gleaning as a way to care for the poor (Ruth 2:1-3).

Glory
Praise and honor. "Fear God and give him glory" (Revelation 14:7). Also, the radiant presence of God. "And we all, who with unveiled faces contemplate the Lord's glory, are being transformed into his image with ever-increasing glory, which comes from the Lord" (2 Corinthians 3:18).

Gnat
A small, two-winged fly that resembles a mosquito. Gnats include both biting and non-biting forms and typically form large swarms. "The LORD said to Moses, 'Tell Aaron, "Stretch out your staff and strike the dust of the ground," and throughout the land of Egypt the dust will become gnats'" (Exodus 8:16).

G

Goat

A hardy, domesticated mammal that has backward-curving horns and (in the case of males) a beard. Goats are kept for their milk and meat and are noted for their lively behavior. "As I was thinking about this, suddenly a goat with a prominent horn between its eyes came from the west, crossing the whole earth without touching the ground" (Daniel 8:5).

God

The Creator and ruler over all. "God is love. Whoever lives in love lives in God, and God in them" (1 John 4:16).

Gold

A yellow precious metal used in jewelry and decoration and to guarantee the value of currencies. "You blind fools! Which is greater: the gold, or the temple that makes the gold sacred?" (Matthew 23:17).

Golden Calf

An idol made by the Israelites when Moses was on Mount Sinai. Moses was furious when he saw it and burned it, ground it to powder, scattered it on the water, and made the Israelites drink it (Exodus 32:20).

Golgotha

Also called Calvary, this was the site immediately outside Jerusalem's walls where Jesus was crucified.

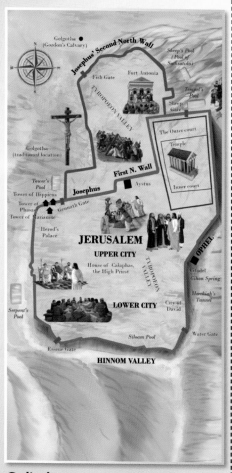

Goliath

A giant Philistine warrior defeated by the young David, the future king of Israel (1 Samuel 17).

Gomer

The unfaithful wife of the prophet Hosea (Hosea 1:2-3; 3:1-3). Hosea's relationship with Gomer paralleled the relationship between God and the unfaithful people of Israel. Even though Gomer ran away from Hosea to be with another man, he loved her and forgave her. In the same way, God continued to love His people even when they worshipped other gods, and He did not abandon His covenant with them.

Gomorrah

A city that was so wicked, God destroyed it with fire and burning sulfur. He saved Lot, Abraham's nephew, but Lot's wife looked back and became a pillar of salt (Genesis 19:26).

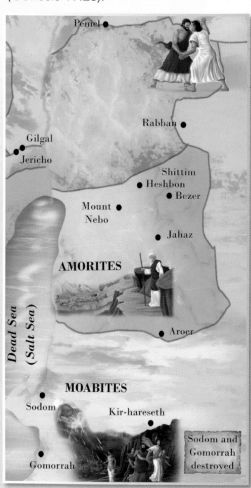

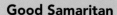

G

Good Samaritan

When a lawyer asks Jesus, "Who is my neighbor?" Jesus tells the parable of the good Samaritan (Luke 10:25-37). In it, a traveler is stripped of his clothing, beaten, and left to die on the roadside. First a priest and then a Levite pass by, but both avoid the man. Finally, a Samaritan sees him and offers his help even though Samaritans and Jews were usually enemies. Jesus then made His point:

"'Which of these three do you think was a neighbor to the man who fell into the hands of robbers?'

"The expert in the law replied, 'The one who had mercy on him.'

"Jesus told him, 'Go and do likewise.'"

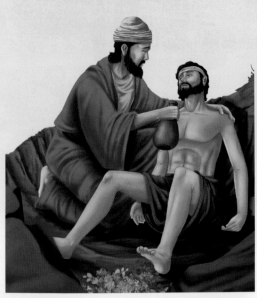

Goshen

The area in Egypt in the eastern delta of the River Nile. It was given to the Hebrews by Pharaoh in Genesis 45:9-10, and the Hebrews stayed there until the Exodus.

Gospel

The good news of salvation through Jesus Christ. "This gospel of the kingdom will be preached in the whole world as a testimony to all nations, and then the end will come" (Matthew 24:14). The word also refers to the first four books of the New Testament—Matthew, Mark, Luke, and John.

Grace

The free and unmerited favor of God. God shows His grace by saving and blessing imperfect people. "Let us then approach God's throne of grace with confidence, so that we may receive mercy and find grace to help us in our time of need" (Hebrews 4:16).

Grapes

Vineyards were symbols of prosperity in Old Testament times. "Then each of you will eat fruit from your own vine and fig tree and drink water from your own cistern" (2 Kings 18:31). "When you harvest the grapes in your vineyard, do not go over the vines again...Leave the remaining grapes for the foreigners, orphans, and widows" (Deuteronomy 24:21).

Habakkuk

The eighth of the twelve Old Testament minor prophets. The book of Habakkuk was probably composed in the late seventh century BC. The central message, "the righteous person will live by his faithfulness" (2:4), is referred to in Romans 1:17, Galatians 3:11, and Hebrews 10:38.

Hagar

An Egyptian handmaid of Sarah, who gave her to Abraham. She is the mother of Abraham's firstborn son, Ishmael, the father of the Ishmaelites (Genesis 16).

Haggai

One of the twelve Old Testament minor prophets and one of the three who ministered among the Jews who returned from exile to Jerusalem. His book encourages the people to examine their priorities and to build a temple in God's honor in spite of local and official opposition.

H

Haman

A vizier in the Persian Empire under King Ahasuerus (traditionally identified as Xerxes I). In a jealous rage, he tried to have all the Jews in the Persian Empire killed. Mordecai and Esther foiled his plot, and Haman was hanged on the gallows he had erected for Mordecai.

Hannah

The wife of Elkanah and the mother of Samuel (1 Samuel 1).

Hate

Intense dislike. "Hate evil, love good; maintain justice in the courts" (Amos 5:15). On the other hand, "anyone who hates a brother or sister is a murderer, and you know that no murderer has eternal life residing in him" (1 John 3:15).

Healing

Jesus pointed to His healing miracles as signs of His true identity as the Messiah. "Go back and report to John what you hear and see: The blind receive sight, the lame walk, those who have leprosy are cleansed, the deaf hear, the dead are raised, and the good news is proclaimed to the poor" (Matthew 11:5).

Heaven

The home of God, the angels, and those who have been reconciled with God through Christ. "God raised us up with Christ and seated us with him in the heavenly realms in Christ Jesus" (Ephesians 2:6).

Hebrew People

Israelites—the descendants of the patriarchs Abraham, Isaac, and Jacob.

Hebrews

An anonymous New Testament book urging Christians to persevere in the face of persecution and to trust in the teachings of Christ and in His role as mediator between God and humanity.

Hell

A spiritual realm of evil and suffering, traditionally depicted as a place of perpetual fire beneath the earth where the wicked are punished after death. "God did not spare angels when they sinned, but sent them to hell, putting them in chains of darkness to be held for judgment" (2 Peter 2:4).

Herod the Great

The king of Judea when Jesus was born. In the nativity story, King Herod is portrayed as an evil tyrant who killed all the baby boys of Bethlehem who he believed could eventually challenge his rule.

Herodias

A princess of Judaea. Her first husband was the son of Herod the Great. She divorced him and married Herod Antipas. John the Baptist was killed at her request.

Hezekiah

The son of King Ahaz and the thirteenth king of Judah. Hezekiah is one of the most prominent kings of Judah mentioned in the Bible.

H

Hittites
A Canaanite nation. Their ancestor, Heth, is said to be a son of Canaan, son of Ham, son of Noah.

Holy
Sacred. "The altar will be most holy, and whatever touches it will be holy" (Exodus 29:37).

Holy Spirit
The third person of the Trinity—the Spirit of God active in the world. "The Advocate, the Holy Spirit, whom the Father will send in my name, will teach you all things and will remind you of everything I have said to you" (John 14:26).

Honest
Truthful. "An honest answer is like a kiss on the lips" (Proverbs 24:26).

Hope
Confidence that something will happen or that someone is trustworthy. "May the God of hope fill you with all joy and peace as you trust in him, so that you may overflow with hope by the power of the Holy Spirit" (Romans 15:13).

Horses
In the Bible, horses are sometimes symbols of power and strength. "The armies of heaven were following him, riding on white horses and dressed in fine linen, white and clean" (Revelation 19:14).

Hosea
The first of the 12 Old Testament minor prophets. God directed Hosea to marry an unfaithful woman as a demonstration of God's faithful love for unfaithful Israel.

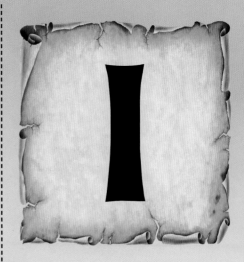

I

Iconium
Now called Konieh, Iconium was the capital of Lycaonia in Asia Minor. It was a large, rich city, 120 miles north of the Mediterranean Sea at the foot of the Taurus mountains. The apostles Paul and Barnabas preached there.

Injustice
Lack of fairness or justice. "Better a little with righteousness than much gain with injustice" (Proverbs 16:8).

Inn
A pub which, in some cases, provided overnight accommodation. "She gave birth to her first-born son and wrapped him in swaddling cloths, and laid him in a manger, because there was no place for them in the inn" (Luke 2:7 RSV).

Iron
A strong, hard, magnetic, silver-gray metal used to make tools, weapons, and building materials. "As iron sharpens iron, so one person sharpens another" (Proverbs 27:17).

Isaac
The second son of Abraham and the father of Jacob and Esau.

Isaiah
The first of the major prophets in the Old Testament. Isaiah ministered in the southern kingdom of Judah, speaking out against corrupt leaders and calling for social justice. His book includes one of the most famous prophecies of the Messiah (9:1-2,6-7).

Ishmael
The first son of Abraham, born to his wife's handmaiden, Hagar.

Israel
Another name for Jacob, son of Isaac, son of Abraham, and a patriarch of the Israelites. Jacob's 12 sons became the fathers of the 12 tribes of the nation of Israel.

Issachar
The ninth of Jacob's 12 sons and the father of the Israelite tribe of Issachar.

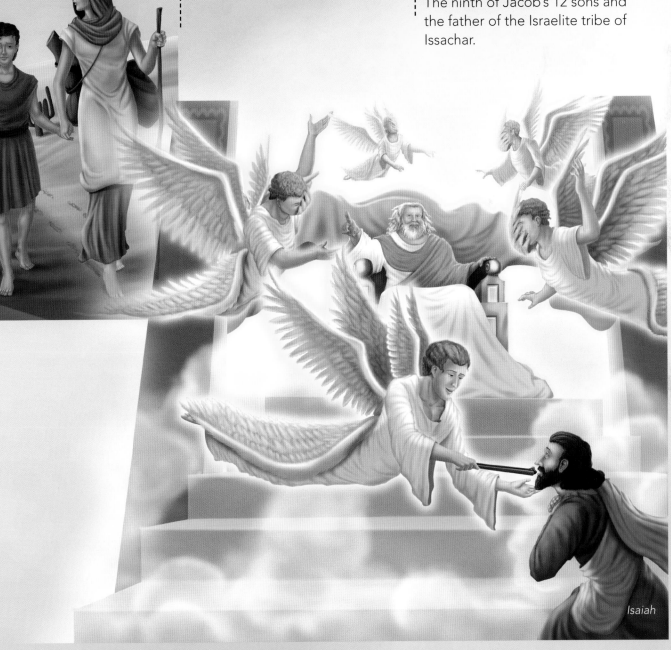

Isaiah

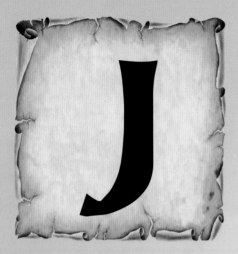

Jabin

The name of two kings of Hazor (Joshua 11:1-14; Judges 4:23-24).

Jacob

Another name for Israel, son of Isaac, son of Abraham, and a patriarch of the Israelites. Jacob's 12 sons became the fathers of the 12 tribes of the nation of Israel.

Jael

The heroine who killed Sisera, commander of a Canaanite army, in order to deliver Israel from the troops of King Jabin (Judges 4:17-24).

Jairus

A patron of a synagogue in Galilee who asked Jesus to heal his 12-year-old daughter. Jesus went to Jairus's house and restored the little girl to life.

James

In the Gospels, James is the brother of John. James, John, and Peter are Jesus's three closest friends. Early in the book of Acts, James is martyred for his faith. The New Testament book of James was written by another James—the half-brother of Jesus—who believed in Jesus as the Christ only after Jesus rose from the dead.

Jason

Jason of Tarsus was an early Jewish convert to Christianity. He lived in Thessalonica and provided refuge for the apostle Paul, Silas, and Timothy (Acts 17:5-9).

Jehoiakim

The king of Judah from 608 to 598 BC. He was the eldest son of King Josiah. His birth name was Eliakim.

Jehoshaphat

The name of at least three people in the Old Testament:

- A scribe in King David's court (2 Samuel 8:16).
- One of King Solomon's district governors (1 Kings 4:17).
- The king of Judah who is famous for winning a battle in a unique way: He "appointed men to sing to the LORD and to praise him for the splendor of his holiness" and positioned them at the head of the army (2 Chronicles 20).

Jehu

The tenth king of the northern kingdom of Israel. He is noted for zealously executing judgment on the house of wicked King Ahab—and for driving his chariot like a maniac (2 Kings 9:20).

Jephthah

One of Israel's judges who led the Israelites in battle against Ammon. Jephthah made a foolish vow to sacrifice to the Lord whatever came out of his house when he returned home. Sadly, that turned out to be his daughter (Judges 11).

Jeremiah

The second major prophet of the Old Testament, sometimes referred to as "the weeping prophet." He is traditionally credited with writing the books of Jeremiah (the longest book in the Bible) and Lamentations. Jeremiah ministered during the destruction of Jerusalem by the Babylonians in 587 BC.

Jehoshaphat

Jericho

Jericho, the City of Palms, is situated on the west side of the Jordan River. After Jerusalem, it is the most excavated site in Israel. The most famous story about Jericho is that of the walls falling down in Joshua 6.

Jesse

The grandson of Ruth and Boaz and the father of King David.

Jesus; Jesus of Nazareth; Jesus Christ

The Son of God and the awaited Messiah prophesied in the Old Testament.

Jethro

Moses's father-in-law—a Kenite shepherd and priest of Midian.

Jezebel

The wife of wicked King Ahab of Israel. She led the people to worship false gods and opposed the great prophet Elijah.

Jeroboam

The first king of the northern kingdom of Israel after the ten northern Israelite tribes revolted against Rehoboam, son of Solomon (1 Kings 12).

Jerusalem

The ancient city west of the Dead Sea, the capital of the Old Testament kingdom of Judah, and the city where Jesus was crucified. During its long history, Jerusalem was destroyed at least twice, besieged 23 times, attacked 52 times, and captured and recaptured 44 times.

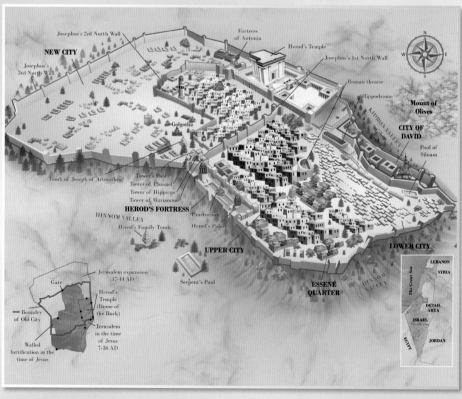

Joash

A king of Judah. When his grandmother, Athaliah, murdered the royal family so she could become queen, the baby Joash was hidden for six years. He became king at age seven and reigned for forty years. He is also known for repairing Solomon's temple, which was in disrepair (2 Kings 11–12).

Job

The central figure of the book of Job. He was a blessed man who lived righteously in the land of Uz. His faith was tested through the most difficult circumstances imaginable. The book of Job, a long poem in which his friends incorrectly blame him for his difficulties, debunks the idea that bad things never happen to good people. The name Job is the English translation of the Hebrew name *Iyov* which means "persecuted, hated."

Joel

The second of the 12 Old Testament minor prophets. The apostle Peter quoted the book of Joel on the Day of Pentecost (Acts 2:14-21).

John

One of the 12 apostles, the brother of the apostle James, and the author of the Gospel of John, the letters of 1, 2, and 3 John, and the book of Revelation. Christian tradition holds that John outlived all the other apostles and was the only one not to die a martyr's death (with the exception of Judas Iscariot, who committed suicide). John's Gospel was written long after the other three Gospels and emphasizes Jesus's identity as the Son of God.

John Mark

An assistant to Paul and Barnabas on their missionary journeys. He deserted them on their first missionary journey, but he later ministered with Barnabas and was eventually reconciled with Paul (2 Timothy 4:11). He is believed to be the author of the Gospel of Mark.

John the Baptist

Jesus's cousin and a Jewish preacher who used baptism to call Israel to repentance and prepare the way for Jesus's ministry. John the Baptist is the one who called Jesus "the Lamb of God" (John 1:29,36). He was executed during Jesus's ministry by Herod Antipas.

Joash

J

Jonah

The fifth of the 12 Old Testament minor prophets. In the book of Jonah, Jonah ran away from God's call on his life but had a change of heart after being swallowed by an enormous sea creature.

Jonathan

The eldest son of King Saul, a heroic soldier (1 Samuel 14), and a close friend of King David (1 Samuel 19:1).

Joppa

A town where Peter raised Tabitha (Dorcas) from the dead (Acts 9:36-42). While there, Peter had a vision that led him to preach the gospel to Gentiles for the first time (Acts 10).

Jordan River

The Jordan River flows south from Mount Hermon, on the border between Syria and Lebanon, through northern Israel to the Sea of Galilee. It continues south, eventually emptying into the Dead Sea. Joshua led Israel across the Jordan to enter the Promised Land, and John the Baptist baptized Jesus in the Jordan.

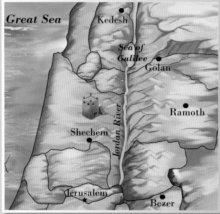

Joseph

In the Old Testament, Joseph is Jacob's favorite son. Sold into slavery by his jealous brothers, he goes on to become the second-most powerful man in Egypt after Pharaoh. In the New Testament, Joseph is the husband of Mary, the mother of Jesus.

Joshua

The leader of the Israelite tribes after the death of Moses. The book of Joshua tells the story of the Israelites' invasion of Canaan, their conquest, and the division of land under Joshua's leadership.

Josiah

Josiah became king of Judah at the age of eight after the assassination of his father, King Amon. He reigned for 31 years and instituted many reforms.

Joy

A feeling of great pleasure and happiness. "Clap your hands, all you nations; shout to God with cries of joy (Psalm 47:1).

Judah

The fourth son of Jacob and Leah and the father of the Israelite tribe of Judah. When the nation of Israel divided in two, Judah was the name of the southern kingdom. The Messiah was expected to be a descendant of Judah (Genesis 49:10). Jesus was from the tribe of Judah and is called "the Lion of the tribe of Judah, the Root of David" in Revelation 5:5.

Judas Iscariot

One of the 12 original disciples of Jesus Christ. He is known for his betrayal of Jesus to the Sanhedrin for 30 silver coins.

Judas, son of James

In some New Testament passages, Judas son of James appears among the list of the 12 apostles, but in others, Thaddaeus appears instead. These were likely the same person.

Jude

Brother of the author of the book of James, and Jesus's half-brother. His one-chapter New Testament letter is the second-to-last book of the Bible.

Judge

Old Testament judges were leaders in Israel before Saul was chosen as Israel's first king.

Judges

The Old Testament book of Judges contains the history of 12 of Israel's leaders after Joshua died but before Saul was chosen as Israel's first king. The judges were by no means perfect.

Judgment

Christians are encouraged to judge between disputes in the church (1 Corinthians 6:1) but not to make a practice of pointing out people's faults (Matthew 1:1-5). The apostle Paul writes, "If we were more discerning with regard to ourselves, we would not come under [God's] judgment" (1 Corinthians 11:31).

Julius

A centurion of the cohort of Augustus whom Festus, governor of Judea, ordered to take the apostle Paul to Rome. Julius had great regard for Paul and allowed him to land at Sidon and visit his friends there. In a later part of the voyage he saved the apostle from other soldiers (Acts 27:1-44).

Justice

Fair behavior or treatment. "Follow justice and justice alone, so that you may live and possess the land the Lord your God is giving you" (Deuteronomy 16:20).

Josiah instituted reforms.

Rome

Three Taverns

Appii Forum

Puteoli

Pompeii

ITALIA

Brundisium

Tarentum

Luke joins Paul

MACEDONIA

Phili

Amphipolis

Thessalonica

Berea

AEG

SE

Larissa

Delphi

Messina

Rhegium

SICILY

Syracuse

Olympia

ACHAIA

Corinth

Ath

Cenchrea

Sparta

Paul speaks to the Areopagus

Malta

Phoenix

Cauda

F

The Great Sea

Cyrene

Syrtis Major

CYRENAICA

Paul's Missionary Journeys

Black Sea

Sinope

RACE

Paul restores young
Eutychus to life

Heracleia

BITHYNIA
AND PONTUS

Paul resumes
his missionary
travels

Byzantium

polis

Ancyra

ASIA

GALATIA

Tavium

Troas

Adramyttium

Assos

Ancyra

Parnassus

Pergamos

Mitylene

Thyatira

Sebaste

CAPPADOCIA

Paul and Barnabas
mistaken for gods

Pergamum

Sardis

Archelais

Smyrna

Philadelphia

Tripolis

Laodicea

CILICIA

Ephesus

Seleucia

Miletus

Cremna

Lystra

Cnidus

LYCIA

Perga

Derbe

Tarsus

Myra

Antioch

Rhodes

Salmone

Salamis

TE

CYPRUS

SYRIA

Lasea

Proconsul
Sergius Paulus
converted

Paphos

avens

Porcius Festus
sends Paul to Rome
to appeal to Caesar

Sidon

Damascus

Tyre

Caesarea

Jerusalem
Conference
AD 49

Antipatris

Jerusalem

JUDEA

Alexandria

EGYPT

Memphis

N

River Nile

← Paul's first missionary journey
← Paul's second missionary journey
← Paul's third missionary journey
← Paul's voyage to Rome

W   E

S

K

Kingdom of Heaven

The home of God, the angels, and those who are reconciled to God through Christ. Also, God's reign on earth. "From that time on Jesus began to preach, 'Repent, for the kingdom of heaven has come near'" (Matthew 4:17).

Korah

The leader of a rebellion against Moses (Numbers 16:21). This story also appears in the Koran and is referred to in Jude 11.

King

A male ruler of an independent state, especially one who inherits his position by right of birth.

King

Laban
The son of Bethuel, son of Nahor, nephew of Abraham. Laban's sister, Rebekah, is the wife of Isaac (Genesis 24). Jacob, one of the sons of this marriage, flees to Laban's house and eventually marries his daughters, Leah and Rachel.

Lamentations
A collection of poetic laments for the destruction of Jerusalem, traditionally thought to have been written by the prophet Jeremiah.

Lamp
As a lamp gives light, so God provides guidance. "You, LORD, are my lamp; the LORD turns my darkness into light" (2 Samuel 22:29). In the New Testament, believers are encouraged, "You are the light of the world. A town built on a hill cannot be hidden. Neither do people light a lamp and put it under a bowl…Let your light shine before others, that they may see your good deeds and glorify your Father in heaven" (Matthew 5:14-16).

Last Supper
The final meal that Jesus shared with His apostles in Jerusalem before His crucifixion.

Law
In the Bible, the Law includes the Ten Commandments and all the stipulations God gave the Israelites through Moses. "This observance will be for you like a sign on your hand and a reminder on your forehead that this law of the LORD is to be on your lips. For the LORD brought you out of Egypt with his mighty hand" (Exodus 13:9).

The New Testament teaches that people are made right with God by grace through faith, not by trusting in the Law (Galatians 2:16).

Lazarus
The brother of Mary and Martha. Jesus restored Lazarus to life four days after Lazarus had died (John 11).

Leah
The first of Jacob's two wives and the mother of six of his twelve sons, the fathers of the twelve tribes of Israel. Jacob also married Leah's younger sister, Rachel.

The Last Supper

Leprosy

The Bible words translated "leprosy" were used for various contagious skin diseases that sometimes caused discoloration, lumps, and in severe cases, disfigurement and deformities. Lepers were social outcasts in Bible times. Jesus broke with social customs by touching a leper to heal him (Matthew 8:1-3).

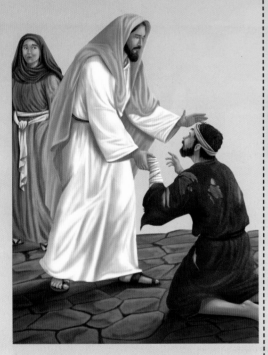

Levi

The third son of Jacob and Leah, and the father of the Israelite tribe of Levi (the Levites).

Levites

Members of the Israelite tribe of Levi. Levites were originally responsible for ministering in the tabernacle and the temple.

Leviticus

Moses wrote the book of Leviticus between 1440 and 1400 BC. The central theme is God's holiness and His requirement of holiness in the Israelites.

Lion

In the Bible, a lion is sometimes a symbol of royalty and power. "The Lion of the tribe of Judah, the Root of David, has triumphed" (Revelation 5:5).

Locusts

A large, flying grasshopper. Locusts are solitary creatures, but from time to time the population explodes and they migrate in vast swarms, causing tremendous damage to vegetation. The eighth Egyptian plague involved locusts: "The LORD said to Moses, 'Stretch out your hand over Egypt so that locusts swarm over the land and devour everything growing in the fields, everything left by the hail'" (Exodus 10:12).

Lord's Supper

Holy Communion—the sacrament instituted at the Last Supper that commemorates Jesus's death.

Lot

The nephew of Abraham. Abraham rescued Lot and his family from invading armies. Later, God saved Lot and his family from the destruction of Sodom and Gomorrah, but Lot's wife turned to look back at the falling city and was immediately turned into a pillar of salt.

M

Love

God's nature, which He manifests to us and develops in us. "God is love. Whoever lives in love lives in God, and God in them" (1 John 4:16)

Luke

The author of the Gospel of Luke and the Acts of the Apostles—more content than any other New Testament writer, even the apostle Paul. He traveled with Paul but was not an apostle himself. He was the only New Testament writer who was not a Jew.

Lying

Telling untruths and falsehoods. "A lying tongue hates those it hurts, and a flattering mouth works ruin" (Proverbs 26:28).

Lystra

A city in central Anatolia, which is now part of present-day Turkey. Paul ministered there and met Timothy, who would become his protégé.

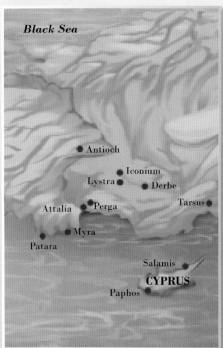

Macedonia

A mountainous nation north of Greece. The history of Paul's first journey through Macedonia is described in Acts 16:10–17:15.

Malachi

The last of the twelve Old Testament minor prophets and one of the three who ministered after the exile. The book of Malachi addresses the lax religious and social behavior of the Israelites, whose commitment to God had, once again, begun to wane. Malachi predicted that before the day of the Lord, Elijah would return to "turn the hearts of the parents to their children, and the hearts of the children to their parents" (4:6).

Malta

A small island in the Mediterranean where Paul and 275 others ran aground on their way to Rome (Acts 27:27-44).

Manasseh

The first Manasseh mentioned in the Bible was one of Joseph's sons and the father of the Israelite tribe of Manasseh. Hundreds of years later, another Manasseh became king of the southern kingdom of Judah at the age of 12 and reigned for 55 years (2 Kings 21:1; 2 Chronicles 33:1).

Manger

A long trough from which animals feed. "This will be a sign to you: You will find a baby wrapped in cloths and lying in a manger" (Luke 2:12).

M

Manna

A bread-like substance that God miraculously provided for the Israelites to eat during their 40-year desert wanderings (Exodus 16). The word sounds like the Hebrew word for "What is it?"

Manoah

Samson's father (Judges 13), an Israelite from the tribe of Dan.

Mark

(See John Mark.) The Gospel of Mark is the second book of the New Testament and the first of the four Gospels to be written. Nearly all of Mark is included in Matthew and in Luke. It tells of the ministry of Jesus from His baptism to His death, burial, and resurrection.

Mars Hill

The Roman name for a hill in Athens, Greece, also called the Areopagus. Paul delivered a famous sermon there (Acts 17:19-23), addressing the religious idolatry of the Greeks, who had even built an altar to an unknown god. He quoted Greek philosophers while teaching his listeners how they could be reconciled to God.

Martha

Sister of Mary and Lazarus. They lived in the village of Bethany, near Jerusalem, where Jesus raised Lazarus from the dead. Mary and Martha are contrasted in Luke 10:38-42.

Martha

Mary

These are the three most prominent women in the Bible named Mary:

- The wife of Joseph and the virgin mother of Jesus Christ, who was conceived within her by the Holy Spirit
- Mary Magdalene, one of Jesus's followers who witnessed His crucifixion and resurrection
- The sister of Martha and Lazarus, who "sat at the Lord's feet listening to what he said" (Luke 38:39).

Matthew

Also known as Levi, Matthew was a dishonest tax collector whose life was changed when Jesus chose him as one of His disciples (Mark 2:14). The Gospel of Matthew is the first book of the New Testament. It includes many Old Testament references and demonstrates that Jesus is the Messiah.

Matthias

Matthias was chosen to replace Judas Iscariot after Judas's betrayal of Jesus and subsequent suicide (Acts 1:15-26).

Medes

An ancient people who lived in what is now northwestern Iran. Together with the Persians, the Medes overthrew the Babylonian Empire.

M

Mediterranean Sea

An intercontinental sea bordered by the Atlantic Ocean on the west, Asia on the east, Europe on the north, and Africa on the south.

Mephibosheth

There are two men by the name of Mephibosheth in the Bible, and both appear in 2 Samuel. One was a son of King Saul whom David delivered to be hanged in retaliation for his father's slaughter of a band of Gibeonites (2 Samuel 21:1-9). The other was a crippled grandson of King Saul. When King David had conquered all of Israel's enemies, he remembered the family of his friend Jonathan and brought Jonathan's son Mephibosheth and his infant son Mika to Jerusalem, where they "always ate at the king's table" (2 Samuel 9).

Mercy

Compassion or forgiveness. "Once you were not a people, but now you are the people of God; once you had not received mercy, but now you have received mercy" (1 Peter 2:10).

Meshach

One of three Jewish men thrown into a fiery furnace by Nebuchadnezzar, king of Babylon, when they refused to bow down to his image. All three were preserved from harm (Daniel 3).

Mesopotamia

An ancient region in the eastern Mediterranean that included the Tigris and Euphrates river systems. It is known as "the cradle of civilization" because it is the first place where complex urban centers grew. Abraham traveled from Mesopotamia to Canaan. Today this area is mostly in Iraq but includes parts of modern-day Kuwait, Iran, Syria, and Turkey.

Micah

One of the 12 Old Testament minor prophets and a contemporary of Isaiah, Amos, and Hosea. He prophesied in Judah from about 737 to 696 BC. The book of Micah includes this famous verse: "What does the LORD require of you? To act justly and to love mercy and to walk humbly with your God" (6:8).

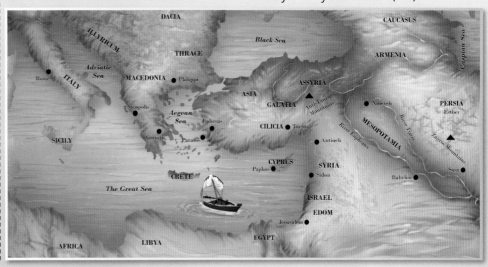

M

Micaiah
A prophet who predicted the defeat and death of Ahab, king of Israel (1 Kings 22; 2 Chronicles 18).

Michal
A daughter of King Saul and the first wife of King David.

Midianites
Descendants of Abraham and his wife Keturah. Moses's father-in-law was a Midianite. The Midianites were often opposed to the Israelites. Gideon and his band of 300 men defeated an entire Midianite army (Judges 7).

Midwife
A person, typically a woman, who is trained to assist women in childbirth. Hebrew midwives Shiphrah and Puah saved infant Hebrew boys from the king of Egypt (Exodus 1:15-21).

Minister
To serve. In the Old Testament, the word often refers to service in the tabernacle and the temple. In the New Testament, it often refers to those who serve the Lord (1 Timothy 4:6) by preaching the new covenant (2 Corinthians 3:6).

Miriam
The elder sister of Moses and Aaron. Miriam saved Moses's life at his birth, arranged for his care as a child, and helped him lead the Israelites from Egypt to the Promised Land.

Moab
A mountainous strip of land in modern-day Jordan that lies along much of the eastern shore

of the Dead Sea. The Moabites were often opposed to the Israelites.

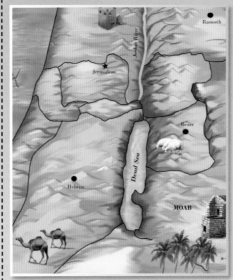

Money
The Bible warns against the love of money (1 Timothy 6:6-10) and encourages generosity (Proverbs 19:17).

Mordecai
The cousin and guardian of Esther. Mordecai played a key role in saving the Israelites from destruction—an event reported in the book of Esther and celebrated at the festival of Purim.

Moses
Born a Hebrew, raised as an Egyptian prince, exiled as a fugitive, and finally chosen to lead the Exodus from Egypt and to receive the Law of God, Moses was the most important Jewish prophet.

Mount Ararat
Genesis 8:4 indicates that Noah's ark came to rest on the mountains of Ararat.

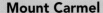

M

Mount Carmel
A coastal mountain range in northern Israel, stretching from the Mediterranean Sea toward the southeast. The prophet Elijah defeated the prophets of the false god Baal there (1 Kings 18:16-40).

Mount Hermon
A mountain cluster that straddles the border between modern-day Syria and Lebanon. It may have been where Jesus was transfigured, though Mount Tabor is the traditional location.

Mount Hor
The location where Moses's brother, Aaron the high priest, died (Numbers 33:38).

Mount Moriah
The mountain range where Abraham traveled to sacrifice his son Isaac at God's command (Genesis 22:1-18). God eventually stopped Abraham and provided a ram for him to sacrifice instead. Some scholars believe Moriah was also the site of the Jewish temple.

Mount of Olives
A mountain ridge near Jerusalem's Old City, named for the olive groves that once covered its slopes. Several key events related in the Gospels and the book of Acts took place on the Mount of Olives, including Jesus's ascension into heaven.

Mount Sinai
Also called Horeb, Sinai is a mountain in the Sinai Peninsula of Egypt where Moses received the Ten Commandments.

Mount Tabor
The site in northern Israel where Barak (under the leadership of the Israelite judge Deborah) defeated the army of Jabin, commanded by Sisera, in the mid-twelfth century BC. It is believed by many Christians to be where Jesus was transfigured (Matthew 17:1-9).

Mount Tabor

Mourning
Deep sorrow. "'He will wipe every tear from their eyes. There will be no more death' or mourning or crying or pain, for the old order of things has passed away" (Revelation 21:4).

Music
In the Old Testament, music was included in worship at the temple. "All these men were under the supervision of their father for the music of the temple of the LORD, with cymbals, lyres and harps, for the ministry at the house of God" (1 Chronicles 25:6). Many of the psalms were set to music. In the New Testament, believers are encouraged, "Be filled with the Spirit, speaking to one another with psalms, hymns, and songs from the Spirit. Sing and make music from your heart to the Lord" (Ephesians 5:18-20).

The Great Sea

GOSHEN

Raamses (Tanis)

Plague of frogs

Succoth

Etham

The

Pithom

Lake
Timsah

Bitter L

EGYPT

Heliopolis

Migdol

Gizeh

Pi-hahi

Memphis

Baal-
zephon

Nile River

Crossing the Red Sea

– – Traditional Route of the Exodus

..... Possible Alternative Routes

Miracle of water
from the rock.
Battle with the
Amalekites

The Exodus of the Israelites

* Horeb is an alternative
name for Mount Sinai

Moses dies after he sees the Promised Land from Mt. Nebo. Joshua leads the Israelites into Canaan.

Ai

Bethel

Jericho

Ashdod

Jerusalem

Mt Nebo

Plain of Philistia

Lachish

Dibon

Dead Sea

Gaza

CANAAN

Hebron

Arnon River

Moab

Beer-sheba

The Negeb

ay to the Land of the Philistines

Spies in Canaan

WILDERNESS OF SHUR

Kadesh-barnea

Oboth

Punon

The Way to Shur

Israelites wander in the wilderness for 40 years

The King's Highway

Wilderness of Zin

Scapegoat

EDOM

arah

Wilderness of Paran

Bronze snake

Elath

Ezion-geber

SINAI

Elim

MIDIAN

The golden calf

Dophkah

Hazeroth

Alash

Gulf of Aqabah

Rephidim

Mt Sinai * (Mt Horeb)

N

Moses receives the Ten Commandments

W

f Suez

S

ed Sea

55

M

Mustard Seed

One of the smallest seeds in agriculture, the mustard seed grows into a large tree. "The kingdom of heaven is like a mustard seed…though it is the smallest of all seeds, yet when it grows, it is the largest of garden plants" (Matthew 13:31-32). "If you have faith as small as a mustard seed, you can say to this mountain, 'Move from here to there,' and it will move. Nothing will be impossible for you" (Matthew 17:20).

Myrrh

A fragrant gum resin obtained from certain trees and used in perfumes, medicines, and incense, especially in the ancient Near East. Myrrh was one of the gifts given to baby Jesus by the wise men (Matthew 2:11).

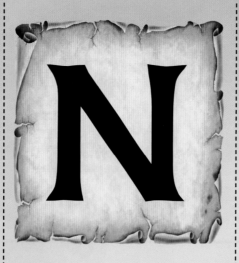

Naaman

A leper and commander of the Syrian army who was cured of his leprosy by the prophet Elisha. "Go, wash yourself seven times in the Jordan, and your flesh will be restored and you will be cleansed" (2 Kings 5:10).

Naboth

The owner of a plot of land on the hill of Jezreel that King Ahab wanted to buy. Naboth could not sell it because he inherited the land from his father. Ahab's wife, Jezebel, plotted to kill Naboth by mock trial so that her husband could take possession of the land after his death (1 Kings 21).

Nahum

One of the 12 Old Testament minor prophets. Nahum foresaw the end of the Assyrian Empire and the destruction of its capital city, Nineveh. The book of Nahum was probably written in Jerusalem in the seventh century BC.

N

Naomi

The wife of Elimelech and mother-in-law of Ruth. Naomi and Elimelech moved from their home in Judea to Moab to escape famine. After the deaths of her husband and sons, Naomi returned to Bethlehem with Ruth, who refused to be parted from her. Ruth was King David's great-grandmother.

Naphtali

The sixth son of Jacob and father of the Israelite tribe of Naphtali.

Nathan

A prophet in King David's court and one of his closest advisors. Nathan prompted David's confession of his sin with Bathsheba (2 Samuel 12:1-14).

Nazareth

A historic city in lower Galilee (northern Israel). It was Jesus's boyhood home, but the people there rejected His teaching. Jesus responded by noting, "A prophet is not without honor except in his own town and in his own home" (Matthew 13:57), and He moved His base of operations to Capernaum.

Nebuchadnezzar

The ruler of the Neo-Babylonian Empire from about 605 to about 562 BC. He built the beautiful Hanging Gardens of Babylon, and he destroyed Jerusalem and the temple and took the Israelites away as exiles.

Nehemiah

The governor of Judea under Artaxerxes I of Persia. The book of Nehemiah describes his campaign to rebuild the walls of Jerusalem under great opposition. The accounts are punctuated by his prayers: "Remember me with favor, my God, for all I have done for these people" (Nehemiah 5:19).

New Heavens and New Earth

The eternal home of God's people. "See, I will create new heavens and a new earth. The former things will not be remembered, nor will they come to mind" (Isaiah 65:17). "Then I saw 'a new heaven and a new earth'" (Revelation 21:1).

Nehemiah

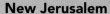

N

New Jerusalem

The eternal city of God's people. "I saw the Holy City, the new Jerusalem, coming down out of heaven from God, prepared as a bride beautifully dressed for her husband. And I heard a loud voice from the throne saying, 'Look! God's dwelling place is now among the people, and he will dwell with them. They will be his people, and God himself will be with them and be their God'" (Revelation 21:2-3).

New Testament

The second part of the Christian Bible. Originally written in Greek, the New Testament records the life and teachings of Christ and His earliest followers. It includes the four Gospels, the Acts of the Apostles, 21 letters by the apostle Paul and others, and the book of Revelation.

Nicodemus

A Pharisee and a member of the Sanhedrin mentioned in three places in the Gospel of John:

- He visited Jesus one night to discuss Jesus's teachings (John 3:1-21).
- He reminded his colleagues in the Sanhedrin that the Law required that a person be heard before being judged (John 7:50-51).
- He appeared after Jesus's crucifixion to help Joseph of Arimathea prepare Jesus's body for burial (John 19:39-42).

Nile River

The longest river in the world. It begins south of the equator, flows north through northeastern Africa, and empties into the Mediterranean Sea. The Nile is about 4,132 miles (6,650 kilometers) long and drains an area of about 1,293,000 square miles (3,349,000 square kilometers). In the first Egyptian plague, God turned the waters of the Nile into blood (Exodus 7).

The Nile River

Nineveh

The capital city of the Neo-Assyrian Empire. Nineveh was located in modern-day northern Iraq on the eastern bank of the Tigris River. God sent Jonah to preach to the Ninevites of their coming destruction. But when the inhabitants fasted and repented, God was merciful and spared the city. In 722 BC, the Assyrians completed their conquest of the northern kingdom of Israel and repopulated the land.

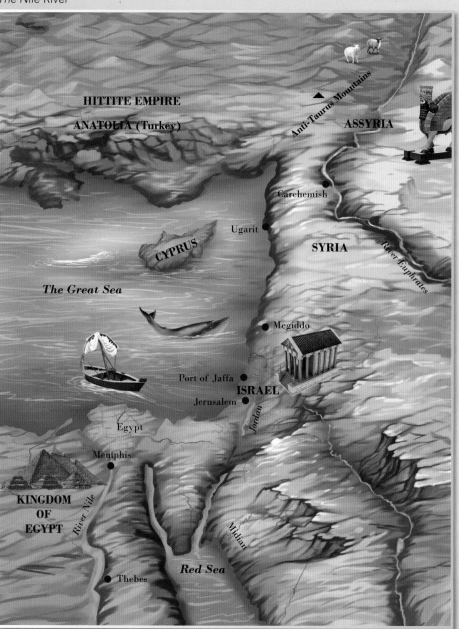

N

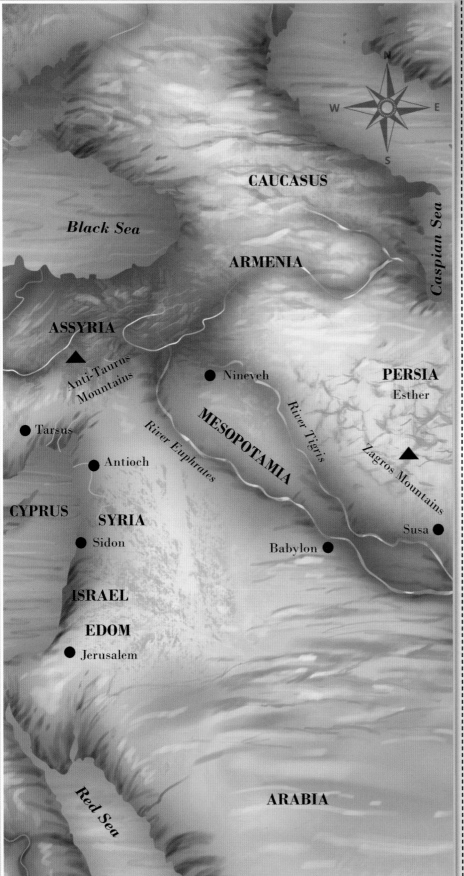

CAUCASUS

Black Sea

ARMENIA

Caspian Sea

ASSYRIA

Anti-Taurus Mountains

● Nineveh

PERSIA

Esther

● Tarsus

MESOPOTAMIA

River Euphrates

River Tigris

Zagros Mountains

● Antioch

CYPRUS

SYRIA

Babylon ●

Susa ●

● Sidon

ISRAEL

EDOM

● Jerusalem

Red Sea

ARABIA

Noah

The builder of an ark (boat) in which he, his family, and two animals of every species survived the great flood (Genesis 5–8).

Numbers

The fourth of the five books of Moses. In it, God promises the Israelites that they shall become a great nation, that they will have a special relationship with God, and that they will take possession of the land of Canaan.

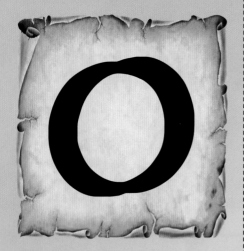

Obadiah

One of the 12 Old Testament minor prophets. The one-chapter book of Obadiah, a prophecy against the nation of Edom, is the shortest book in the Old Testament. The Edomites were the descendants of Esau, and the Israelites descended from his twin brother, Jacob. A quarrel between the two brothers affected their descendants for many hundreds of years.

Obedience

The act of following instructions given by someone in authority. "Through him we received grace and apostleship to call all the Gentiles to the obedience that comes from faith for his name's sake" (Romans 1:5).

Old Testament

The first part of the Christian Bible, consisting of 39 books, most of which were written in Hebrew (some in Aramaic) between about 1200 and about 300 BC.

Orpah

The daughter-in-law of Naomi, wife of Chilion, and sister-in-law of Ruth. After the death of her husband, Orpah intends to go to Judea with Naomi and Ruth, but Naomi persuades Orpah to return to Moab.

Orphan

A child whose parents have died. God shows special concern for orphans and other powerless members of society. "Religion that God our Father accepts as pure and faultless is this: to look after orphans and widows in their distress and to keep oneself from being polluted by the world" (James 1:27).

Orpah

P

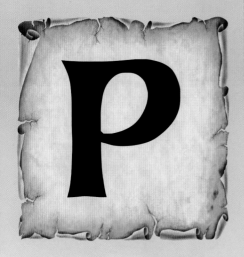

Palm Tree

Leaves of palm trees were sometimes awarded as prizes or viewed as symbols of victory. At the time of Jesus's triumphal entry into Jerusalem, "they took palm branches and went out to meet him, shouting, 'Hosanna! Blessed is he who comes in the name of the Lord! Blessed is the king of Israel!'" (John 12:13).

Parable

A simple story used to illustrate a moral or spiritual lesson. The Gospels record many of Jesus's parables. "Jesus spoke all these things to the crowd in parables; he did not say anything to them without using a parable" (Matthew 13:34).

Passover

A festival that commemorates the Israelites' delivery from slavery in Egypt as described in the Old Testament book of Exodus. God directed the Israelites to put a lamb's blood on the doorposts of their houses. He said that when He judged Egypt, He would see the blood and "pass over" their houses. In the New Testament, John the Baptist referred to Jesus as the Lamb of God—probably a reference to the Passover lamb (John 1:29,36).

Patmos

A small Greek island in the Aegean Sea where John wrote the book of Revelation. "I, John, your brother and companion in the suffering and kingdom and patient endurance that are ours in Jesus, was on the island of Patmos because of the word of God and the testimony of Jesus" (Revelation 1:9).

Paul

Also known as Saul, Paul was an apostle (though not one of the original 12 apostles) who spread the gospel of Christ in the first century AD. He is generally considered to be one of the most important figures of the apostolic age. As a Roman citizen and a Jew, he was able to minister to both audiences. Paul founded several churches in Asia Minor and Europe in the mid-30s to the mid-50s AD. He wrote 13 of the 27 books in the New Testament.

Pentecost

Originally a Jewish festival commemorating God's giving of the Ten Commandments at Mount Sinai. Christians use this day to celebrate the gift of the Holy Spirit and the birth of the church (Acts 2). Pentecost is celebrated on the Sunday 50 days after Easter.

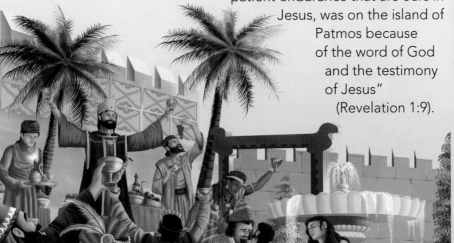

Palm Trees

P

Perga
An ancient Anatolian city in modern Turkey. In 46 AD, the apostle Paul ministered there (Acts 14:25).

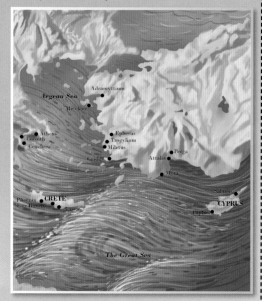

Persecution
Hostility and ill-treatment, especially because of race or political or religious beliefs. "Everyone who wants to live a godly life in Christ Jesus will be persecuted" (2 Timothy 3:12).

Persia
A massive world empire made up of a series of dynasties centered in modern-day Iran. The first of these was established by Cyrus the Great in 550 BC with the conquest of Media, Lydia, and Babylonia. The Israelites had been exiles in Babylon, and Cyrus allowed them to return to Jerusalem (2 Chronicles 36:22-23).

Pharaoh
A ruler in ancient Egypt. "Joseph was thirty years old when he entered the service of Pharaoh king of Egypt" (Genesis 41:46).

Pharisee
A member of an ancient Jewish sect distinguished by strict observance of Jewish tradition and the Law of Moses. "The Pharisee stood by himself and prayed: 'God, I thank you that I am not like other people—robbers, evildoers, adulterers—or even like this tax collector'" (Luke 18:11). The apostle Paul was a Pharisee before he met the risen Christ. The Sanhedrin was made up of Pharisees and Sadducees.

A leader of the Colossian church. The apostle Paul wrote him a New Testament letter, asking him to reconcile with his runaway slave, Onesimus.

Philip
The New Testament mentions several people with this name. One was chosen by Jesus to be one of the 12 apostles. Another was one of the church's first missionaries (Acts 8).

Philippi
An important city founded in the fourth century BC and eventually a Roman colony encompassing some 700 square miles. The apostle Paul established the first European Christian community there during his second missionary journey, which took place between about 49 and 51 AD.

The Persian Empire

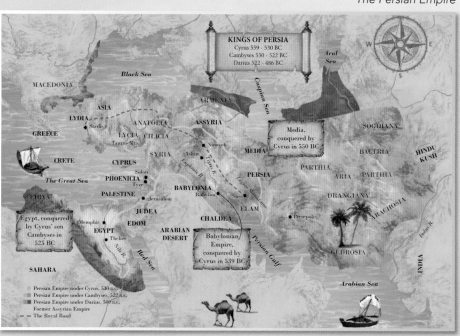

P

Philippians

The apostle Paul's letter to the Philippians is the eleventh book of the New Testament. Paul wrote it from prison, yet it is known as the epistle of joy. "Rejoice in the Lord always. I will say it again: Rejoice!" (Philippians 4:4).

Philistia

The plain on the southwest coast of Palestine, remarkable for the extreme richness of its soil. The Philistines came into conflict with the Israelites during the twelfth and eleventh centuries BC. Palestine is referred to as "the land of the Philistines" in Psalms 60:8, 87:4, and 108:9. In 1 Samuel 17, young David defeats the giant Philistine warrior Goliath.

Phoenicia

An ancient region corresponding to modern-day Lebanon and parts of Syria and Israel. Its inhabitants, the Phoenicians, were notable merchants, traders, and colonizers of the Mediterranean in the first millennium BC.

Pillar of Fire

One of the manifestations of the presence of God in the Old Testament. "By day the LORD went ahead of them in a pillar of cloud to guide them on their way and by night in a pillar of fire to give them light, so that they could travel by day or night" (Exodus 13:21).

Plague

God sent ten plagues on Egypt to persuade Pharaoh to release the Israelites from slavery (Exodus 7–12). Pharaoh finally agreed after the tenth plague, triggering the Exodus.

Pontius Pilate

A Roman prefect (governor) of Judaea under the emperor Tiberius. Pilate presided over the trial of Jesus and ordered His crucifixion.

Potiphar

The captain of the palace guard under Pharaoh, king of Egypt. Joseph, sold into slavery by his brothers, was taken to Egypt and sold to Potiphar as a household slave. Potiphar later made Joseph the head of his household. Potiphar's wife, who is not named in the Bible, falsely accused Joseph of mistreating her. Potiphar put Joseph in prison, but Joseph rose to prominence because of his faithfulness and his ability to interpret dreams.

P

Potter

A person who makes pots, plates, and other objects from clay. God is pictured as a potter in the Old Testament: "You, LORD, are our Father. We are the clay, you are the potter; we are all the work of your hand" (Isaiah 64:8).

Praise

Worship and adoration. "The LORD is my strength and my defense; he has become my salvation. He is my God, and I will praise him, my father's God, and I will exalt him" (Exodus 15:2).

Prayer

A solemn request for help or an expression of thanks addressed to God. "Do not be anxious about anything, but in every situation, by prayer and petition, with thanksgiving, present your requests to God" (Philippians 4:6).

Preach

In the New Testament, this word means to publicly declare the good news of salvation. "From that time on Jesus began to preach, 'Repent, for the kingdom of heaven has come near'" (Matthew 4:17).

Pride

A feeling of deep pleasure or satisfaction derived from someone's achievements, qualities, or possessions. "I take great pride in you. I am greatly encouraged; in all our troubles my joy knows no bounds" (2 Corinthians 4:7). However, pride can distract people from a humble reliance on God. "Pride goes before destruction, a haughty spirit before a fall" (Proverbs 16:18).

Priest

Jewish priests were set apart by God to minister in the temple. The New Testament refers to all of God's people as priests. "You are a chosen people, a royal priesthood, a holy nation, God's special possession, that you may declare the praises of him who called you out of darkness into his wonderful light" (1 Peter 2:9).

Prodigal Son

One of Jesus's most famous parables (Luke 15:11-32). In it, a father has two sons. The younger son asks for his inheritance early and spends it unwisely. He returns to his father's house to ask to be hired as a servant, but his father welcomes him as his son and celebrates his return. When the older son complains and refuses to join in, his father reminds him that one day, the older son will inherit everything. The father explains that they should celebrate the return of the younger son because he was lost and now is found. Jesus used this parable to show why He showed mercy to sinners—because God loves His children even when they stray.

Prayer

Q

Promised Land

The land of Canaan, promised to Abraham and his descendants in Genesis 12:7.

Proverbs

The Old Testament book of Proverbs was chiefly written by King Solomon. It contains short, pithy sayings about moral behavior, wisdom, and the meaning of life. "The fear of the LORD is the beginning of knowledge, but fools despise wisdom and instruction" (Proverbs 4:5).

Psalms

Prayers, poems, and hymns that focus worshippers' thoughts on God in praise and adoration. The Old Testament book of Psalms includes 150 psalms that explore many subjects, including God and His creation, war, worship, wisdom, sin and evil, judgment, justice, and the coming of the Messiah.

Quail

A small, short-tailed game bird. "They asked, and he brought them quail; he fed them well with the bread of heaven" (Psalm 105:40).

Queen of Sheba

A woman of great wealth, beauty, and power. "When the queen of Sheba heard about the fame of Solomon and his relationship to the LORD, she came to test Solomon with hard questions" (1 Kings 10:1). God had granted Solomon the gift of wisdom (1 Kings 3:5-12), so "nothing was too hard for the king to explain to her" (1 Kings 10:3). The queen of Sheba was impressed with Solomon's wisdom, hospitality, wealth, and reputation. The story ends with an exchange of resources and the queen of Sheba returning to her own country. Sheba is believed to have been in modern-day Ethiopia or Yemen.

Quail

Queen of Sheba

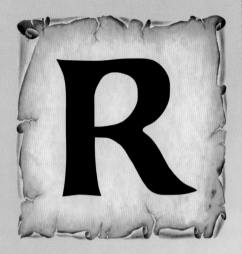

Rachel

The favorite of Jacob's two wives as well as the mother of Joseph and Benjamin, fathers of two of the twelve tribes of Israel. Rachel was the daughter of Laban and the younger sister of Jacob's first wife, Leah.

Rahab

A resident of Jericho who helped the Israelites to capture the city. In the New Testament, she is included in the genealogy of Jesus (Matthew 1:5) and commended for her faith (Hebrews 11:31).

Rainbow

An arch of colors in the sky, caused by the refraction and dispersion of the sun's light by moisture in the atmosphere. The rainbow is a sign of God's promise never to destroy the earth by a flood. "Whenever the rainbow appears in the clouds, I will see it and remember the everlasting covenant between God and all living creatures of every kind on the earth" (Genesis 9:16).

Rebekah

"The daughter of Bethuel son of Milkah, who was the wife of Abraham's brother Nahor" (Genesis 24:15). This makes Rebekah Abraham's great-niece and Isaac's second cousin. She was also Isaac's wife and the mother of Jacob and Esau.

Red Sea

An extension (or inlet) of the Indian Ocean, located between Africa and Asia. Moses led the Israelites through the Red Sea in the exodus from Egypt. "He rebuked the Red Sea, and it dried up; he led them through the depths as through a desert" (Psalm 106:9).

R

Redeem

In the Bible, this word usually means "to buy back." Israelites referred to God as their Redeemer (Psalm 19:14), and Christians proclaim Jesus Christ as the Redeemer. "You know that it was not with perishable things such as silver or gold that you were redeemed from the empty way of life handed down to you from your ancestors, but with the precious blood of Christ, a lamb without blemish or defect" (1 Peter 1:18-19).

Rehoboam

A son of Solomon and the fourth king of Israel after Saul, David, and Solomon. When the ten northern tribes of Israel rebelled to form the independent kingdom of Israel, he remained as king of the southern kingdom of Judah.

Repentance

In the Bible, this word means to turn away from sin and to turn to God. "John the Baptist appeared in the wilderness, preaching a baptism of repentance for the forgiveness of sins" (Mark 1:4).

Resurrection

The rising of Christ from the dead and the rising of all the dead at the last judgment. "If we have been united with him in a death like his, we will certainly also be united with him in a resurrection like his" (Romans 6:5).

Reuben

The first son of Jacob and Leah and the father of the Israelite tribe of Reuben.

Revelation

In the Bible, a revelation is a divine or supernatural disclosure to humans of something they could not have known otherwise. "I did not receive it from any man, nor was I taught it; rather, I received it by revelation from Jesus Christ" (Galatians 1:12). The book of Revelation is a collection of images that depict God's victory over evil.

Israelite Tribe of Reuben

R

Righteousness

Moral rightness. "This righteousness is given through faith in Jesus Christ to all who believe" (Romans 3:22).

Roman Empire

The Roman Empire included most of what would now be considered Western Europe. First-century Jews hoped the Messiah would deliver them from Roman domination.

Ruth

Ruth is a Moabitess. She marries one of the sons of the Hebrew family of Elimelech and Naomi, whom she meets when they leave Bethlehem to escape a famine. Elimelech and his two sons die, leaving Naomi and her two daughters-in-law as widows. When Naomi decides to return to Bethlehem, Ruth promises to go with her, despite the fact that Orpah, Naomi's other daughter-in-law, returns instead to her home.

Romans

The apostle Paul wrote his New Testament letter to the church at Rome to explain that salvation is by grace through faith in Jesus Christ.

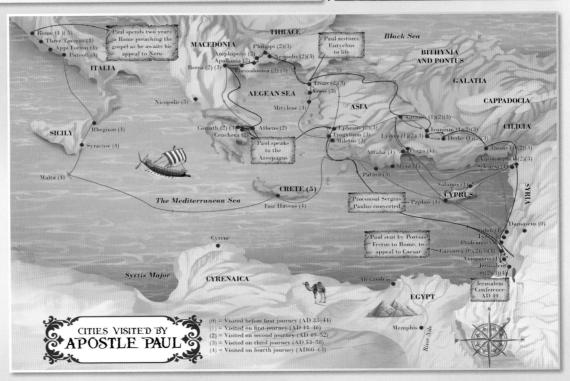

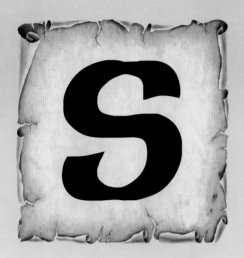

Sabbath

A day of religious observance and rest from work, kept by Jews from Friday evening to Saturday evening. "For in six days the LORD made the heavens and the earth, the sea, and all that is in them, but he rested on the seventh day. Therefore the LORD blessed the Sabbath day and made it holy" (Exodus 20:11).

Sacrifice

Giving up an animal or a possession as an offering to God. "Christ loved us and gave himself up for us as a fragrant offering and sacrifice to God" (Ephesians 5:2).

Sadness

Sorrow and unhappiness. "Weeping may stay for the night, but rejoicing comes in the morning" (Psalm 30:5).

Sadducees

A member of a Jewish sect at the time of Jesus that denied the resurrection of the dead, the existence of spirits, and much of the Hebrew Bible. Most of the Sadducees were members of the upper class. The Sanhedrin included Sadducees and Pharisees. "The Sadducees, who say there is no resurrection, came to him with a question" (Matthew 22:23).

Samaria

In the Old Testament, Samaria is the capital of the northern kingdom of Israel. In the New Testament, Samaria is the central region of Israel, bordered by Galilee in the north and Judaea in the south. In the west was the Mediterranean Sea, and on the east, the Jordan River. Samaritans were hated by first-century Jews, yet Jesus made a Samaritan the hero of one of his most famous parables (Luke 10:25-37), and He ministered to a Samaritan woman near the well of Sychar (John 4:1-26).

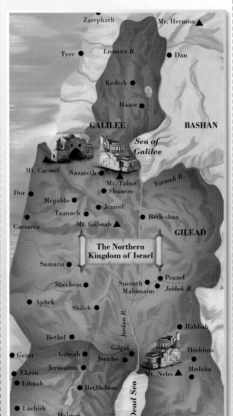

The Northern Kingdom of Israel

Samson

A legendary Israelite warrior and judge, famous for his awesome strength and poor judgment (Judges 13–16).

Samuel

One of Israel's greatest prophets and leaders. He anointed Saul and David as kings of Israel.

S

Sanhedrin

In the time of the New Testament, the Sanhedrin was the highest Jewish council. It consisted of 71 members. The Sadducees outnumbered the Pharisees in the Sanhedrin, but the Pharisees may have had more control because they had the support of the people. The Sanhedrin condemned Jesus to death and imprisoned the apostles.

Sapphira

Ananias and his wife, Sapphira, were members of the early Christian church in Jerusalem. They both died suddenly after lying to the Holy Spirit about money (Acts 5).

Sarai / Sarah

Sarah, originally called Sarai, was the wife and also the half-sister of Abraham. Her only son, Isaac, was born when she was about 90 years old.

Satan

Satan ("enemy" or "adversary") is a deceiver who uses cunning and temptation to lead humanity astray. "Your enemy the devil prowls around like a roaring lion looking for someone to devour. Resist him, standing firm in the faith" (1 Peter 5:8-9). "The great dragon was hurled down—that ancient serpent called the devil, or Satan, who leads the whole world astray" (Revelation 12:9).

Saul

The first king of Israel. He was anointed by the prophet Samuel in response to Israel's demand for a king, but he lost favor with God because of his disobedience, and David became king. In the New Testament, Saul is another name for the apostle Paul.

Savior

In the Bible, this word describes God (see Psalm 68:19) and often Jesus Christ in particular. "We wait for the blessed hope—the appearing of the glory of our great God and Savior, Jesus Christ" (Titus 2:13).

Scapegoat

On the Day of Atonement, the high priest's responsibilities included sending a goat—the scapegoat—into the wilderness to bear the sins of the people (Leviticus 16).

Scriptures

The sacred writings of Judaism and Christianity contained in the Bible. "All Scripture is God-breathed and is useful for teaching, rebuking, correcting, and training in righteousness" (2 Timothy 3:16).

S

Sea of Galilee

A large freshwater lake in Israel also known as Kinneret, Lake of Gennesaret, or Lake Tiberias. It is fed partly by underground springs, though its main source is the Jordan River, which flows through it from north to south. This is where Jesus walked on the water (Matthew 14:22-33) and calmed the storm (Mark 4:35-41).

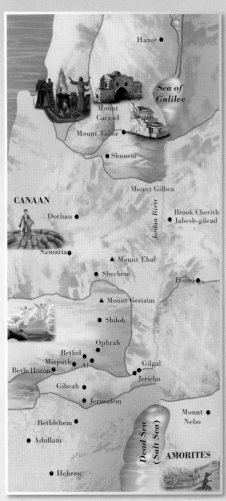

Serpent

Genesis 3 pictures a serpent tempting Eve and instigating the fall of humankind. Revelation 12:9 identifies the serpent as Satan.

Shadrach

One of three Jewish young men thrown into a fiery furnace by Nebuchadnezzar, king of Babylon, when they refused to bow down to his image. All three were preserved from harm (Daniel 3).

Sheep

The Bible refers to the people of God as sheep. "Know that the LORD is God. It is he who made us, and we are his; we are his people, the sheep of his pasture" (Psalm 100:3). "My sheep listen to my voice; I know them, and they follow me" (John 10:27).

Shepherd

The Bible uses this word to describe God. "The LORD is my shepherd, I lack nothing. He makes me lie down in green pastures, he leads me beside quiet waters, he refreshes my soul" (Psalm 23:1-3). It also describes those who are responsible to care for God's people. "Be shepherds of God's flock that is under your care, watching over them" (1 Peter 5:2).

Sermon on the Mount

The Sermon on the Mount (Matthew 5–7) is the longest continuous section of Jesus's teachings found in the New Testament. It includes Jesus's radical reinterpretation of the Jewish Law and some of His best-known teachings, such as the Beatitudes and the Lord's Prayer.

S

Shield

God is sometimes called a shield because He protects His people. "My God is my rock, in whom I take refuge, my shield and the horn of my salvation" (2 Samuel 22:3). Paul also includes a shield in his description of the armor of God. "Take up the shield of faith, with which you can extinguish all the flaming arrows of the evil one" (Ephesians 6:16).

Ship

The most famous ships in the Old Testament include Noah's ark (Genesis 6–8) and the ship that Jonah was thrown from (Jonah 1). In the New Testament, Jesus walked on water to a boat (Matthew 14:22-33) and calmed a storm while in a boat (Mark 4:35-41). A ship that carried the apostle Paul toward Rome ran aground on the Mediterranean island of Malta (Acts 27–28).

Silas

Silas, or Silvanus, was a leading member of the early Christian community who accompanied the apostle Paul on parts of his first and second missionary journeys.

Shiloh

An ancient city near the middle of Israel. It was a major religious center before the first temple was built in Jerusalem. "The whole assembly of the Israelites gathered at Shiloh and set up the tent of meeting there" (Joshua 18:1).

Sidon

The third-largest city in Lebanon, situated on the Mediterranean coast about 25 miles (40 kilometers) north of Tyre and the same distance south of the capital, Beirut. Sidon is also the name of a son of Canaan, son of Noah (Genesis 10:15).

Simeon

Jacob's second son and the father of the Israelite tribe of Simeon. In the New Testament, Simeon is a "righteous and devout" man who offers a blessing when he meets Mary, Joseph, and the baby Jesus in the temple (Luke 2:22-35).

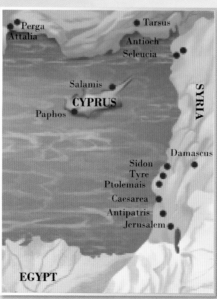

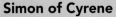

S

Simon of Cyrene

The man forced by the Romans to carry Jesus's cross on the way to His crucifixion (Matthew 27:32).

Simon Peter

One of Jesus's 12 apostles. He and James and John appear to be Jesus's closest friends, and Peter is sometimes the spokesman for the apostles (Matthew 16:13-16; Acts 1:15; 2:14, for example). Shortly before the crucifixion, he denied knowing the Lord, but Jesus restored their relationship after the resurrection. Peter was the first apostle to preach the gospel (Acts 2) and the first to preach to Gentiles (Acts 10). Two New Testament letters bear his name.

Simon the Leper

Simon the Leper was hosting Jesus at his home in Bethany when a woman anointed Jesus's head with expensive perfume (Matthew 26:6-13).

Sin

Hebrew and Greek words commonly translated "sin" in the Bible mean "miss the mark." "If you do what is right, will you not be accepted? But if you do not do what is right, sin is crouching at your door; it desires to have you, but you must rule over it" (Genesis 4:7). "If we confess our sins, he is faithful and just and will forgive us our sins and purify us from all unrighteousness" (1 John 1:9).

Sisera

A commander of the Canaanite army of King Jabin of Hazor. He was defeated by the Israelite tribes of Zebulun and Naphtali, led by Barak and Deborah, and was killed by Jael, who hammered a tent peg into his temple (Judges 4).

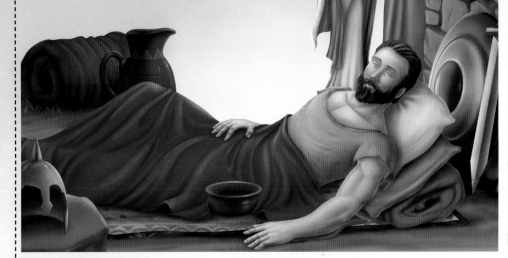

Slavery

The Old Testament laws regarding slavery set a high moral standard (Deuteronomy 15:12-18; 24:17-22). The New Testament figuratively depicts believers as being delivered from slavery to sin so they might become slaves to God (Roman 6:19-23).

Sodom

Sodom and Gomorrah were wicked cites that God destroyed with burning sulfur (Genesis 19:24).

Sodom

S

Solomon

The third king of Israel, son of King David, and builder of the first temple in Jerusalem. Solomon possessed greater wisdom, wealth, and power than his predecessors. Ultimately, however, he was a human being with failings, which led him into sin. Solomon's sins led to the division of his kingdom during the reign of his son Rehoboam.

Son of God

Jesus Christ is the only Son of God (Matthew 14:33). In a lesser sense, those who believe in Him are also called children of God (Romans 8:14-17).

Son of Man

Jesus is referred to as the Son of Man 88 times in the New Testament. As well as being the Messiah and fully God (John 1:1), He was also a human being (John 1:14). "This is how you can recognize the Spirit of God: Every spirit that acknowledges that Jesus Christ has come in the flesh is from God" (1 John 4:2).

The term is partly a reference to Daniel 7:13-14: "There before me was one like a son of man, coming with the clouds of heaven. He approached the Ancient of Days and was led into his presence. He was given authority, glory and sovereign power; all nations and peoples of every language worshiped him. His dominion is an everlasting dominion that will not pass away, and his kingdom is one that will never be destroyed."

Song of Solomon

The last of the five books of wisdom in the Old Testament, also known as the Song of Songs. It is a lyric poem about the virtues of love between a husband and his wife, thought to have been written by Solomon during the early part of his reign, about 965 BC.

Soul

The immaterial part of a human being. "Take my yoke upon you and learn from me, for I am gentle and humble in heart, and you will find rest for your souls" (Matthew 11:29).

Stairway of Jacob

The connection between the earth and heaven that Jacob dreamed about at Bethel while fleeing from his brother Esau (Genesis 28:10-17).

Solomon

Stephen

The first Christian martyr (Acts 7:54-60). Just before he died, he cried out, "Lord, do not hold this sin against them." Saul of Tarsus (later known as the apostle Paul) was a witness, and Stephen's example may have played a part in Saul's conversion.

Stone Tablets

The two pieces of stone inscribed with the Ten Commandments. There were actually two sets of tablets. The first set was inscribed by God and shattered by Moses when he saw the Israelites worshipping the golden calf. The second set was cut by Moses and rewritten by God. The tablets were stored in the Ark of the Covenant (Hebrews 9:4).

Synagogue

A Jewish house of worship, prayer, and instruction. Synagogue worship was formalized and standardized while the Jews were exiles in Babylon.

Stone Tablets

Syria

Ancient Syria (Aram) was the strip of fertile land lying between the eastern Mediterranean coast and the desert of northern Arabia. The capital of Syria is Damascus.

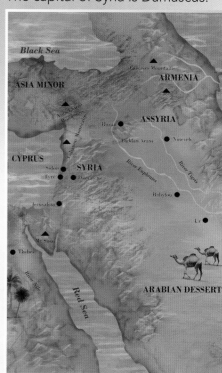

Stairway of Jacob

T

Tabernacle

A portable tent that was used as a place of worship by the ancient Israelites during the wilderness wanderings, the conquest of the Promised Land, and the time of the judges, King Saul, and King David. It was replaced by Solomon's temple.

Tabitha

Also called Dorcas, Tabitha lived in the town of Joppa, a city on the coast of the Mediterranean Sea. Dorcas became sick and died, but Peter brought her back to life.

Tarsus

An ancient city in south-central Turkey with a history stretching back more than 6,000 years. It was the birthplace of the apostle Paul.

GALATIA

CAPPADOCIA

CILICIA

Derbe

Tarsus

Antioch
Seleucia

Salamis

CYPRUS

Paphos

SYRIA

Damascus

Sidon
Tyre
Ptolemais
Caesarea
Antipatris
Jerusalem

Tax

Money that governments collect from citizens to fund public services and projects. When Jesus was asked whether Jews should pay taxes to their Roman oppressors, He replied, "Give back to Caesar what is Caesar's, and to God what is God's" (Luke 20:25).

Tax Collector

In the first century, Jewish tax collectors were deeply unpopular because they worked for the Roman Empire and were often corrupt. Jesus befriended tax collectors, including Zacchaeus and the apostle Matthew.

Tabitha

"While Jesus was having dinner at Matthew's house, many tax collectors and sinners came and ate with him and his disciples" (Matthew 9:10).

Temple

The Jewish house of worship and prayer in Jerusalem. Solomon built the first temple, which the Babylonians destroyed in 587 BC. The Jews built the second temple when they returned from exile, Herod the Great expanded it, and the Romans destroyed it in 70 AD.

The New Testament teaches that believers are now temples of God. "Do you not know that your bodies are temples of the Holy Spirit, who is in you, whom you have received from God? You are not your own; you were bought at a price. Therefore honor God with your bodies" (1 Corinthians 6:19-20).

Temptation

The lure of doing something wrong for personal benefit. "No temptation has overtaken you except what is common to mankind. And God is faithful; he will not let you be tempted beyond what you can bear. But when you are tempted, he will also provide a way out so that you can endure it" (1 Corinthians 10:13).

Ten Commandments

A set of rules that God inscribed on two stone tablets, which He gave to Moses on Mount Sinai (Exodus 20:1-17; Deuteronomy 5:4-21). They form the heart of the Mosaic Law.

Tax Collector

T

Thessalonica

An important port on the Aegean Sea, located at the intersection of two major Roman roads. Paul traveled to Thessalonica with Silas and Timothy on his second missionary journey (Acts 17) and wrote two New Testament letters to the church there.

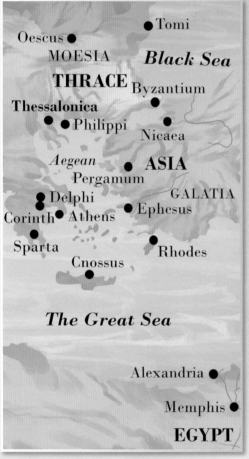

Tomi

Oescus

MOESIA

Black Sea

THRACE

Byzantium

Thessalonica

Philippi

Nicaea

Aegean

ASIA

Pergamum

GALATIA

Delphi

Corinth Athens

Ephesus

Sparta

Rhodes

Cnossus

The Great Sea

Alexandria

Memphis

EGYPT

Thorns

"The soldiers twisted together a crown of thorns and put it on his head" (John 19:2). They did this to Jesus to humiliate Him.

Throne

A chair that symbolizes power and authority. "In the year that King Uzziah died, I saw the Lord, high and exalted, seated on a throne; and the train of his robe filled the temple" (Isaiah 6:1).

Thomas

One of Jesus's 12 apostles. Thomas was not present when Jesus first appeared to the disciples after the resurrection. When told by the others, "We have seen the Lord," Thomas replied that he would not believe them unless he could touch Jesus's wounds. Jesus invited him to do this later, and Thomas exclaimed, "My Lord and my God!" (John 20:24-28).

Thomas

Tigris River

One of the great rivers that flows through Mesopotamia. It joins with the Euphrates, helping to create the Fertile Crescent. The Assyrian capital of Nineveh was located on the Tigris River.

Titus

One of apostle Paul's coworkers and a leader in the church at Crete. Paul wrote a New Testament letter to him.

Tomb

A chamber in which the dead are buried. "There was a violent earthquake, for an angel of the Lord came down from heaven and, going to the tomb, rolled back the stone and sat on it" (Matthew 28:2).

Tower of Babel

In Genesis 11:1-9, the people who lived after the great flood shared one common language and migrated from the east to the land of Shinar. There they agreed to build a city and "a tower that reaches to the heavens." God confused their languages and scattered them all over the world. The tower is a symbol of exaggerated pride and independence from God.

Transfiguration

Christ's shining appearance with Moses and Elijah to three of His disciples. "Jesus took with him Peter, James and John the brother of James, and led them up a high mountain by themselves. There he was transfigured before them. His face shone like the sun, and his clothes became as white as the light. Just then there appeared before them Moses and Elijah, talking with Jesus" (Matthew 17:1-3).

T

Tree of Life

The tree in the Garden of Eden that bore fruit that gave eternal life (Genesis 3:22-24). "In the middle of the garden were the tree of life and the tree of the knowledge of good and evil" (Genesis 2:9). The tree of life reappears in the new Jerusalem (Revelation 22:1-2).

Tree of the Knowledge of Good and Evil

The tree in the Garden of Eden bearing the forbidden fruit that Adam and Eve ate (Genesis 2:9; 3:1-7). "You must not eat from the tree of the knowledge of good and evil, for when you eat from it you will certainly die" (Genesis 2:17).

Triumphal Entry

In Matthew 21:1-11, Mark 11:1-11, Luke 19:28-44, and John 12:12-19, Jesus descends from the Mount of Olives toward Jerusalem, where crowds scatter clothes and palm branches on the ground to welcome Him. Christians celebrate Jesus's triumphal entry into the city on Palm Sunday, a week before Easter Sunday.

Tree of Life

T

Truth

Pontius Pilate rhetorically asked Jesus, "What is truth?" (John 18:38). Jesus had earlier told His disciples, "I am the way and the truth and the life" (John 14:6). He had also told those who believed in Him, "If you hold to my teaching, you are really my disciples. Then you will know the truth, and the truth will set you free" (John 8:32).

Tree of the Knowledge of Good and Evil

Tyre

Tyre, in modern-day Lebanon, is mentioned several times in both the Old and New Testaments. The city was built on a rock island in the Mediterranean Sea.

Triumphal Entry

Black Sea

MACEDONIA

Troy

HITTITES

LYDIA

Athens

Tarsus

CYPRUS

PHOENICIA

CRETE

Sidon

Tyre

The Great Sea
(Mediterranean)

Caesarea

ISRA

Samaria

Joppa

Jer

Jerusalem

PHILISTIA

Dea
Sea

JUDAH

Alexandria

EDOM

THE OLD TESTAMENT WORLD

EGYPT

Sinai
Desert

MIDIAN

Mt Sinai

River Nile

Red Se

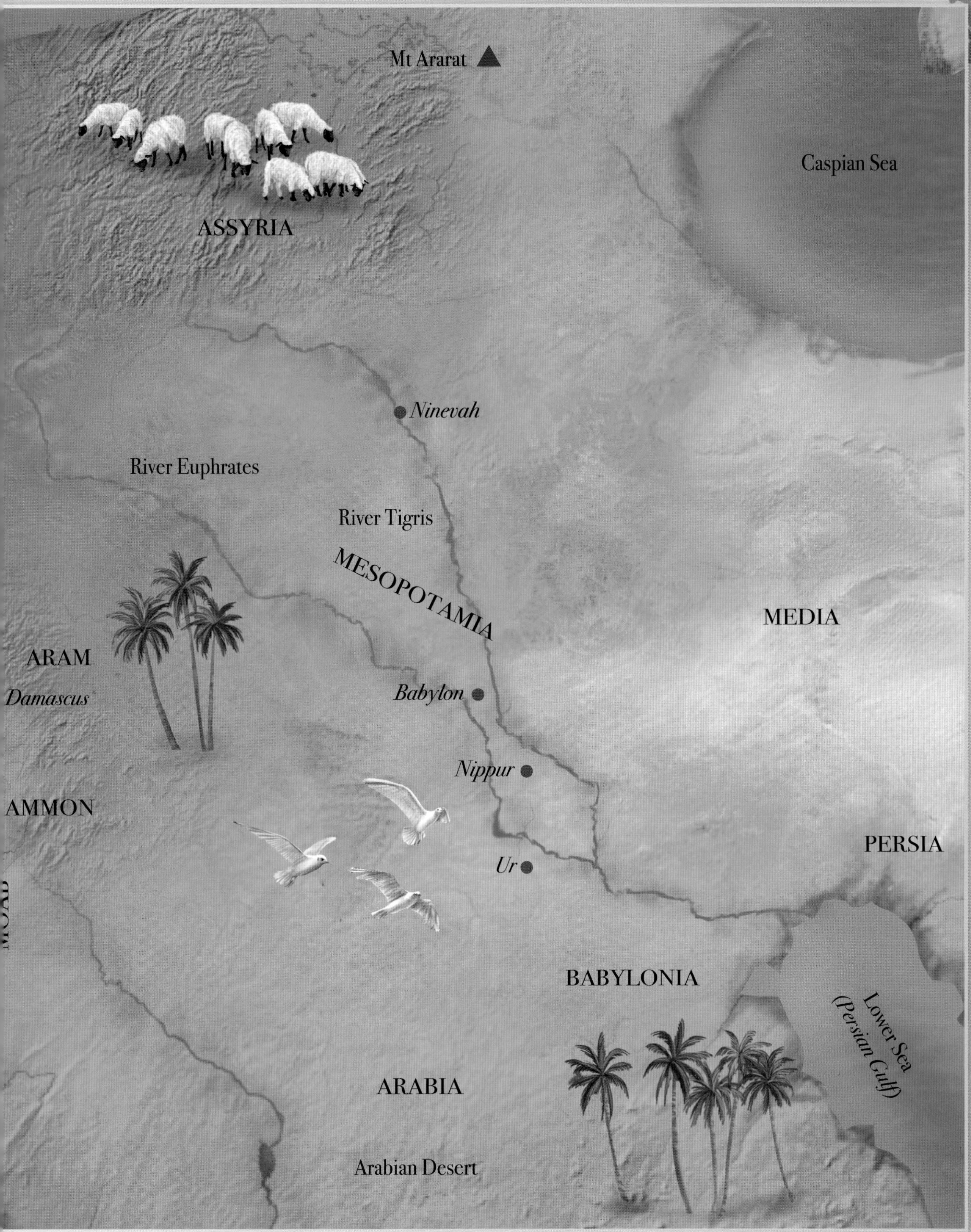

Mt Ararat ▲

Caspian Sea

ASSYRIA

• *Ninevah*

River Euphrates

River Tigris

MESOPOTAMIA

MEDIA

ARAM

Damascus

Babylon ●

Nippur ●

AMMON

PERSIA

Ur ●

BABYLONIA

Lower Sea (Persian Gulf)

ARABIA

Arabian Desert

THE HOLY LAND
IN THE TIME OF
JESUS

ABILENE

Sidon

Damascus

SYRIA

PHOENICIA

Tyre

Caesarea Philippi

GALILEE

TETRARCHY
OF PHILIP

Bethsaida Julias

Capernaum

Bethsaida

Sea of Galilee

Cana

Mt Carmel ▲

Nazareth

Mt
Tabor

DECAPOLIS

Nain

Caesarea

SAMARIA

Samaria

*Shechem
(Sychar)*

The Great Sea
(Mediterranean)

EPHRAIM

PERAEA

Jericho

Emmaus

Bethabara

Jerusalem ▲ Mt of Olives

Bethlehem   *Bethany*

JUDEA

Dead
Sea

NABATAEA

IDUMAEA

U

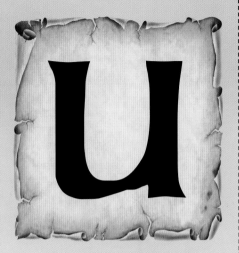

Ur

A city in southern Mesopotamia (modern-day Iraq). Abraham left Ur to settle in the land of Canaan (Genesis 11:31).

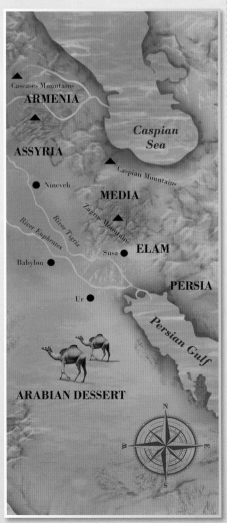

Uriah

A brave and honorable soldier in King David's army. When David fell in love with Uriah's wife, Bathsheba, David had him killed.

Urim and Thummim

Parts of the Jewish high priest's clothing. They may have been sticks or stones—no one knows for sure. "Put the Urim and the Thummin in the breastpiece, so they may be over Aaron's heart whenever he enters the presence of the LORD. Thus Aaron will always bear the means of making decisions for the Israelites over his heart before the LORD" (Exodus 28:30).

Uzziah

Uzziah, also known as Azariah, was a king of Judah. He was 16 years old when he became king and reigned for 52 years. Early in his reign, Uzziah "did what was right in the eyes of the LORD" (2 Kings 15:3). But when the kingdom grew to nearly unprecedented size and wealth, "Uzziah became powerful, [and] his pride led to his downfall" (2 Chronicles 26:16).

V

Valley of Ben Hinnom

A valley below Mount Zion, outside the walls of the Old City of Jerusalem. Before David made Jerusalem the capital of Judah, Canaanites may have used the spot to sacrifice their firstborn children in fire to appease their god Molech. The spot may have also been used as an ever-burning trash heap. A variant of the name (Gehenna) was used for hell.

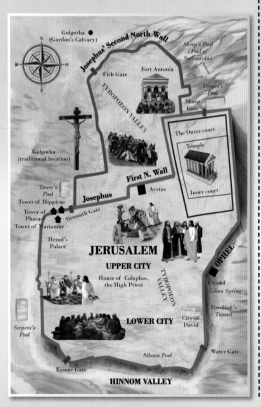

Valley of Dry Bones

A prophetic vision described in Ezekiel 37. Ezekiel saw himself standing in a valley full of dry human bones. The bones connected into human figures and became covered with tissue, flesh, and skin. The vision was a picture of Israel's restoration after the exile in Babylon.

Vashti

The first wife of the Persian king Ahasuerus. According to the book of Esther, Vashti was banished when she refused to show herself to the king's guests at a royal banquet. Ahasuerus then chose Esther to replace her as his wife.

Veil of the Temple

The Most Holy Place—the earthly dwelling place of God's presence—was separated from the rest of the temple by a veil, or curtain, demonstrating mankind's separation from God. When Jesus died, the curtain was torn from top to bottom, announcing humanity's free access to God's presence. "Since we have confidence to enter the Most Holy Place by the blood of Jesus, by a new and living way opened for us through the curtain, that is, his body…let us draw near to God" (Hebrews 10:19-22).

Vine

A vine was a symbol of the nation of Israel (Isaiah 5:1-7). Jesus said, "I am the true vine, and my Father is the gardener. He cuts off every branch in me that bears no fruit, while every branch that does bear fruit he prunes so that it will be even more fruitful" (John 15:1-2). The apostle Paul explained that Gentiles have been grafted into the vine together with Israel (Romans 11:11-24).

W

Well

Jesus was standing by a well when He taught a Samaritan woman about living water. "Whoever drinks the water I give them will never thirst. Indeed, the water I give them will become in them a spring of water welling up to eternal life" (John 4:14).

Wheat

Jesus was probably looking at wheat fields near Sychar when He told His disciples, "The fields are ripe for harvest," referring to the work of spreading the gospel (John 4:34-37). "The harvest is plentiful but the workers are few" (Matthew 9:37). Regarding His own life and crucifixion, He said, "Very truly I tell you, unless a kernel of wheat falls to the ground and dies, it remains only a single seed. But if it dies, it produces many seeds" (John 12:24).

Widow

Widows are given special attention in the Bible. "He defends the cause of the fatherless and the widow, and loves the foreigner residing among you, giving them food and clothing" (Deuteronomy 10:18).

Wilderness

Israel was tempted in the wilderness after the Exodus from Egypt. Jesus was tempted in the wilderness after His baptism and triumphed where Israel had failed (Matthew 4:1-11).

Wine

Jesus's first miracle was to change water into wine at a wedding in Cana of Galilee (John 2:1-12). He later pictured the Pharisees' traditions as old wine and His teachings as new wine that required new wineskins (Luke 5:33-39).

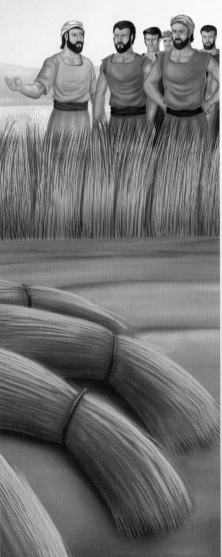

W

Wisdom

Experience, knowledge, and good judgment. Wisdom begins with the fear of the Lord (Proverbs 1:7) and is available to all. "If any of you lacks wisdom, you should ask God, who gives generously to all without finding fault, and it will be given to you" (James 1:5).

Wise Men

The Magi, also referred to as wise men, traveled from the east to worship Jesus shortly after His birth. They brought him gifts of gold, frankincense, and myrrh (Matthew 2:1-12).

Witch of Endor

The witch of Endor is the medium who summons the prophet Samuel's spirit at the demand of King Saul (1 Samuel 28).

Witness

Evidence or proof. "Come now, let's make a covenant, you and I, and let it serve as a witness between us" (Genesis 31:44). Also, a person who sees an event and reports about it. "One of these must become a witness with us of his resurrection" (Acts 1:22).

Woman at the Well

Traveling from Jerusalem in the south to Galilee in the north, Jesus and His disciples took the quickest route through Samaria. Tired and thirsty, Jesus sat by Jacob's well while His disciples went to buy food, and a Samaritan woman came to the well to draw water. During their encounter, Jesus told the woman that He could give her living water (eternal life). When she mentioned that the Messiah would one day explain everything, Jesus replied, "I, the one speaking to you—I am he" (John 4:26).

Worship

The expression of honor and respect to God. "God is spirit, and his worshipers must worship in the Spirit and in truth" (John 4:24).

Wrath

Extreme anger. "A gentle answer turns away wrath, but a harsh word stirs up anger" (Proverbs 15).

X

Yoke

A bar or frame attached to the heads or necks of two work animals (such as oxen) so they can pull a plow or heavy load. Figuratively, it refers to a load someone carries through life. "Come to me, all you who are weary and burdened, and I will give you rest. Take my yoke upon you and learn from me, for I am gentle and humble in heart, and you will find rest for your souls. For my yoke is easy and my burden is light" (Matthew 11:28-30).

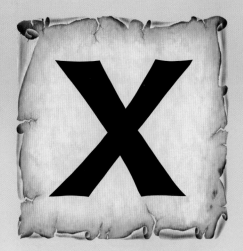

Xerxes I

The fourth king of the (first) Persian Empire. He ruled from 486 BC until his assassination in 465 BC. Xerxes I is most likely the Persian king identified as Ahasuerus in the Book of Esther. He is also known in Western history for his invasion of Greece in 480 BC.

Yahweh

The God of Israel. His name is composed of four Hebrew consonants, Y-H-W-H, which are together known as the Tetragrammaton. God revealed this name to Moses at the burning bush (Exodus 3:13-14), where it is translated "I AM WHO I AM."

Zacchaeus

A chief tax collector at Jericho mentioned only in the Gospel of Luke. Zacchaeus turned from his corrupt ways when Jesus came to his house (Luke 19:1-10).

Zebulun

Jacob's sixth son and the father of the Israelite tribe of Zebulun.

Ten of Jacob's Twelve Sons

Zechariah

The author of the book of Zechariah, the second-to-last book in the Old Testament. Zechariah was one of the twelve Old Testament minor prophets and one of the three prophets who ministered after the Jews' return from exile in Babylon. "I will pour out on the house of David and the inhabitants of Jerusalem a spirit of grace and supplication. They will look on me, the one they have pierced, and they will mourn for him as one mourns for an only child" (Zechariah 12:10).

Zedekiah

The last king of Judah before the destruction of the kingdom by Babylon. Zedekiah refused to accept the counsel of the prophet Jeremiah and rebelled against King Nebuchadnezzar even though Zedekiah had sworn an oath of loyalty to him (2 Chronicles 36:12-13).

Nebuchadnezzar laid siege to Jerusalem in the ninth year of Zedekiah's reign. The city was still under attack two years later, by which time all the food had run out, and Zedekiah tried to escape, only to be captured in the plains of Jericho.

Zephaniah

The great-great-grandson of King Hezekiah who prophesied in the days of Josiah, king of Judah (641–610 BC), living at the same time as the prophet Jeremiah. The book of Zephaniah is the ninth of the 12 minor prophets. "The Lord your God is with you, the Mighty Warrior who saves. He will take great delight in you; in his love he will no longer rebuke you, but will rejoice over you with singing" (Zephaniah 3:17).

Zerubbabel

A Jewish governor of a Persian province and the grandson of Jehoiachin, the second-to-last king of Judah. Zerubbabel led the first group of 42,360 Jews from Babylonian captivity in the first year of Cyrus, King of Persia. Soon afterward he laid the foundation of the second temple in Jerusalem.

Zion

Another name for Jerusalem, which is located near Mount Zion.

Zipporah

The wife of Moses and the daughter of Reuel, or Jethro.

Zerubbabel

Numbered Books of the Bible

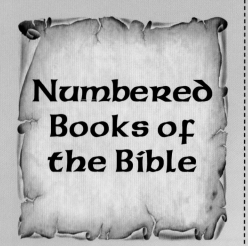

1 and 2 Chronicles

These two books, originally one book, cover the same history as 1 Samuel–2 Kings, but they were written hundreds of years later—after the exile—and from a different perspective. They demonstrate that even though the people had sinned and Jerusalem and the temple had been destroyed, Israel was still the people of God and God would fulfill His promises to them.

1 and 2 Corinthians

The apostle Paul's New Testament letters to the church in Corinth. First Corinthians includes Paul's description of love (chapter 13), one of the most-loved passages in the Bible. It also includes Paul's most detailed teaching on the resurrection (chapter 15).

God's power is channeled through our human frailty: "My grace is sufficient for you, for my power is made perfect in weakness" (12:9).

1, 2, and 3 John

The apostle John wrote these letters between 85 and 95 AD, probably from Ephesus. In 1 John, he warns Christians about the increasing threat of false teachings and encourages them to live in love. The central message of 2 John is that the children of God may abide in the truth, and the truth may abide in them. Third John was written to praise Gaius and Demetrius for their faithful service.

This one-chapter letter is the shortest in the New Testament.

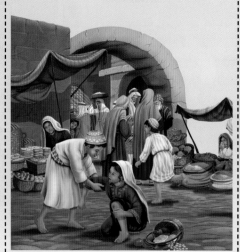

1 and 2 Kings

These two Old Testament books present a history of ancient Israel and Judah from the death of David to the fall of both kingdoms, a period of about 400 years (about 960 to 560 BC). The books of Joshua through 2 Kings are sometimes called the Former Prophets. With 1 and 2 Samuel and 1 and 2 Chronicles, they are sometimes simply called the historical books. Many scholars believe this history was written to explain why Israel and Judah were destroyed.

1 and 2 Peter

The apostle Peter wrote these New Testament letters to all believers of the Christian faith, probably in the 60s AD. His purpose was to strengthen suffering Christians, to encourage them to live as good examples, and to warn them against the increasing number of false teachers attacking the gospel of Jesus Christ.

1 and 2 Thessalonians

The apostle Paul wrote these New Testament letters sometime between 52 and 54 AD. First Thessalonians is one of Paul's earliest letters, written to strengthen and encourage a brand-new church by answering questions about the second coming of Jesus Christ and emphasizing the importance of faith, hope, and love. In 2 Thessalonians, Paul again teaches about the second coming of Jesus Christ, focusing on God's judgment and "the man of lawlessness."

1 and 2 Timothy

The apostle Paul wrote these New Testament letters to Timothy, his "true child in the faith" and the young pastor of the church at Ephesus. In 1 Timothy, written in about 62 AD, Paul offers encouragement and guidelines for effective church leadership. Second Timothy, written in about 67 AD, is probably the last letter Paul wrote. Near the end he writes, "I have fought the good fight, I have finished the race, I have kept the faith" (4:7).

1 and 2 Samuel

These were originally one book, a history written in about 930 BC. In 1 Samuel, we see Israel choosing Saul, the first king, but neglecting and abandoning God. Second Samuel reveals the successes and failures of Israel's second and greatest king—King David.